I0644824

Art Is the Evidence

Art Is the Evidence

A Guide to Art-Based Research

Shaun McNiff

intellect
Bristol, UK / Chicago, USA

First published in the UK in 2026 by
Intellect, The Mill, Parnall Road, Fishponds, Bristol, BS16 3JG, UK

First published in the USA in 2026 by
Intellect, The University of Chicago Press, 1427 E. 60th Street, Chicago, IL 60637, USA

Copyright © 2026 Intellect

All rights reserved. No part of this publication may be reproduced, stored in a retrieval system, or transmitted, in any form or by any means, electronic, mechanical, photocopying, recording, or otherwise, without written permission.

No part of this book may be used or reproduced in any manner for the purpose of training artificial intelligence technologies or systems without written permission from the publisher.

EU GPSR Authorised Representative
LOGOS EUROPE, 9 rue Nicolas Poussin, 17000, LA ROCHELLE, France
E-mail: Contact@logoseurope.eu

A catalogue record for this book is available from the British Library.

Copy editor: MPS Limited
Cover designer: Natalie Thomas, Tanya Montefusco
Cover image: Shaun McNiff, *Piano Player* [detail], 2016. Oil on canvas. 30 in. × 31 in. © Shaun McNiff.
Production manager: Debora Nicosia
Typesetter: MPS Limited

Paperback ISBN 978-1-83595-308-2
ePDF ISBN 978-1-83595-310-5
ePUB ISBN 978-1-83595-309-9

Printed and bound by Halstan

To find out about all our publications, please visit our website. There you can subscribe to our e-newsletter, browse or download our current catalogue and buy any titles that are in print.

www.intellectbooks.com

This is a peer-reviewed publication.

A razor-sharp, crystal-clear and comprehensive account of art-based research which is essential reading for practitioner-researchers everywhere. In affirming that "art is the evidence" within art-based research, this is possibly McNiff's most lucid work to date!

—Ross W. Prior, PhD, Professor Emeritus and Principal Editor of *Journal of Applied Arts & Health*

This book is a timely, authoritative, and deeply accessible guide to the theory and practice of art-based research both within and beyond the academy. Drawing on decades of pioneering experience, Shaun McNiff addresses urgent contemporary questions by illuminating the differences and the connections between artistic and scientific research, and showing how rigorous inquiry can emerge through artistic practice itself.

—Ruth Mateus-Berr, PhD, Professor,
University of Applied Arts Vienna

Highlights from the book

Art offers the space for discovery to emerge naturally, ahead of conscious thought. The gestating process of creation gathers and shapes elements of experience into new insights and expressions. This artistic intelligence is a primary rationale for the existence of applied art disciplines and must be sustained in their research.

The principle of uniqueness characterizes artistic inquiry and together with the physical and sensory character of artistic expression it will inform the discourse about what artificial intelligence can and cannot do.

Art and science are complementary, often intertwined, and sharing many features, but they are different modes of inquiry, and neither can be reduced to, nor justified by, the other.

The most important frontier for free and unfettered art-based research may exist in creative acts and projects happening naturally outside what is currently recognized as research.

"Art is the evidence" within the process of art-based research. The art evidence is empirical and speaks for itself, as it has done convincingly throughout world history, if we can open to its expression. To insist otherwise and require that artistic processes prove their value through something other than themselves and the bounteous physical evidence they generate, is unreasonable.

Contents

Acknowledgments

The practice of art-based research described in this book extends from my work with graduate students over the past 50 years. They instinctively led the way, and I continuously respond. Everything I have learned about artistic intelligence emerged from this cooperation. Hopefully, the following pages will convey the depth and historic continuities of art's contributions to human understanding being revived today throughout the world.

Special thanks to Ross W. Prior for his unwavering support in advancing our shared vision of research through art and for his leadership in founding the *Journal Applied Arts & Health* in 2010 with Intellect Books. The *Journal* has become an invaluable community of international colleagues acting as a slipstream of creation, proving we can go farther and deeper together. In addition to Ross, I am grateful to Catherine Cobb, Gary Nash, Mitchell Kossak, and Ruth Mateus-Berr who also read the manuscript in its early stages and offered insightful reviews. Masoud Yazdani, who established Intellect in 1984 furthered our collective effort when he suggested that I expand a special issue of the *Journal Applied Arts & Health* into a book that became *Art as Research* (2013). Support from Intellect has been sustained in this project by James Campbell, Jessica Lovett, Debora Nicosia, Natalie Thomas, and the team of copy editors and designers.

As I emphasize in the book, I extend sincere gratitude to the challenges, obstacles, opposing positions, and what I consider problematic practices, requirements, and standards that reliably energize the crucible of creation. They have served as inspiration and guides. As Rainer Maria Rilke said, I am afraid that if my demons and struggles leave, "my angels will take flight as well."

Preface: To research through the making of art

It has been 28 years since the publication of *Art-Based Research* (1998), to my knowledge the first book on the subject, and 50+ years since I began to supervise thesis projects related to art and human understanding while shaping my own experience with artistic inquiry. As I described in the earlier book, formal practice of art-based research, with the understanding that the word *art* includes all forms of artistic expression, evolved through my work with students creating theses to culminate their graduate studies integrating all forms of art in therapy and other areas of health, education, and human development. The book explored artistic inquiry in relation to the art therapy field's increasing focus on research and unexpectedly reached a larger audience. Responses came from diverse disciplines and professions, confirming a shared interest and the potential breadth of artistic inquiry.

In this *art-based research redux*, I reflect upon doing, advising, developing, and studying art as research in response to worldwide interest. What has been learned, and what is recommended going forward? What are the fundamental principles, issues, and practices informing the far-ranging possibilities of artistic inquiry?

Simply stated, art-based research, like the art process, is infinitely variable and tied to how people doing the research approach artistic inquiry. This book strives to tersely present why and how this can be done, and how the different methods of inquiry share common artistic elements. The process is closer to straightforward scientific experimentation than the voluminous array of current social science research systems, with their accompanying concepts and procedures being extended now to incorporate art.

When asked, "what is the audience for this book?" my most immediate concern is the academic and professional context where formal research is conducted—especially applied art fields expected to justifying themselves through something other than art. Students at all levels and their faculty advisors need support and clarification as to the nature of art-based research, how it can be done and why, what it offers, and how it complements other forms of inquiry. I also hope to engage those establishing research policy and make the case for artistic inquiry as essential to the larger context of knowledge.

All academic domains, including science, potentially share an interest in how the art process can inform what they do. Ideally, the audience will include psychology, healthcare, education, and other areas open to exploring artistic dimensions of their ongoing practice. The humanities, particularly literature and history, can benefit by reconnecting to their art base and the presentation of research in artistically engaging texts. And the fine arts, design, and architecture have longstanding and flourishing traditions that I consider to be integral to the complete community of research through art.

Ultimately, the practice of every life discipline can be viewed as art and engage artistic inquiry. It is important to reach artists of all types together with general readers interested in artistic intelligence and its fundamental, but often overlooked, place in human understanding. The situations described here ideally suggest bonds between art and all of life.

Among the features distinguishing artistic inquiry is the principle of uniqueness characterizing the personal nature of artistic expression. This quality, and the explication of artistic intelligence, as the foundation of art-based research emerged unplanned from the process of writing this book—both of which, together with the physical and sensory character of artistic expression will inform the discourse about what artificial intelligence can and cannot do. As I emphasize in the following pages, artists consistently study the art of others, not to replicate but to create and then sustain their distinctive ways of working. This is a core value of art and not necessarily current academic and professional research dealing with human experience. The latter, unlike transformative natural science—which shares many qualities with art—tends to follow institutionally accepted and often standardized formats. They approach artistic expressions as *data* to be analyzed and reduced to a pre-existing conceptual framework.

We find ourselves in a context today where those bringing artistic expression to the various applied art fields are expected to validate what they do through *evidence-based* research. While supporting the primacy of evidence in research and decision-making, we can question how it is defined.

There is an assumption and insistence that the evidence is exclusively generated by social science procedures and consequently research concerning artistic processes and outcomes is expected to be conducted within frameworks other than art. In contrast, I maintain that *art is the evidence* within the process of art-based research. The art evidence is empirical and speaks for itself, as it has done convincingly throughout world history if we can open to its expression. To insist otherwise and require that artistic processes prove their value through something other than themselves and the bounteous physical evidence they generate is unreasonable.

The expectation that research in the various applied art areas *will* follow procedures that imitate the natural sciences, together with the often-disparaging characterization of art-based research as self-absorbed, has generated productive tensions. They have encouraged my focus on paradigm clarification and the articulation of how the personal nature of artistic inquiry is ideally paired with a purpose that transcends it in striving to be of use to others.

Since current art-based research primarily involves formal studies within academic and professional settings, I will address the issues and challenges we face in developing approaches that differ from prevailing assumptions about the nature of research. A major objective of this book will be to share what I have learned in helping advisees successfully pursue artistic inquiry within this context, and as I hope to show, many positive outcomes have resulted from dealing with its prevailing requirements and expectations. A concern will be how formal research may more fully engage the creative process, which like nature, is often unpredictable and does not operate according to plans.

Considerable attention will be given to relatively unexplored natural art experimentation (McNiff, 2021a, 2023a). Natural experiments in science and art reflect the formative forces of nature. They share the absence of controlled procedures established in advance and respond to what manifests itself naturally, also described as spontaneously, organically, unexpectedly, wondrously, and as I hope to illustrate here, artistically.

Where science has appreciated and conceptualized this dimension of research, artistic inquiry can too, especially since natural experiments align so closely with nature's creation and improvisations. It can be said that if the process of inquiry is not natural and unique, it is not art. This realization has convinced me that planned and formal art-based research must anticipate and respond to the intuitive and often unexpected processes of creative expression. And most importantly, our discussion of artistic intelligence and inquiry must go beyond academic research to fully understand its potential, therefore carefully studying the ongoing and ubiquitous natural art experiments happening in the world.

Now, and throughout history, writers, playwrights, performing artists, composers, filmmakers, painters, poets, and art-makers in various disciplines engage the spectrum of issues and challenges of human experience. Yet we generally do not include these inquiries in definitions of research intended to generate knowledge, perfect professional practice, and improve life conditions.

Major forms of artistic inquiry I observe happening now and in the past were not necessarily intended to be "research" as it is narrowly defined today, and therefore, an objective of this book is an expansion of the idea and discipline of research to include them.

The following discussion of foundations and guiding principles presents a *raison d'être* of art-based research as it emerged through my work dealing with how art heals—years before the formal implementation of the discipline. It is followed by an account of how I began to develop the idea of art as research, always insisting that it is not a new creation since it sustains what artists have always done and continue to do.

Since art-based research is conducted through art made by the persons conducting the inquiry, my history enables me to present *primary sources* versus *secondary* reflection on what others have done. This hopefully offers an illustration that is consistent with the essential nature of artistic inquiry, as I will discuss later in relation to firsthand experimentation with practice. The description of art-based research taking shape in my work suggests how the broader and more inclusive discipline shares features and a common purpose while manifesting itself through infinitely different ways in keeping with the nature of art. This principle has been validated by the research conducted by the many graduate students I have advised over the years.

I want to emphatically say that this book is neither suggesting nor describing particular methods of practice other than engaging art and its multitude of possibilities to respond to various life conditions, questions, and research directions. It is an artist's guide. Readers are hopefully supported in creating their distinctive ways of pursuing artistic inquiry, in sync with the personal nature of artistic intelligence rather than adopting fixed systems or attempting to mimic what others do.[1] Where some might find this approach blurring lines between art and research, I perceive it as affirming their integral relationship.

Discussion of defining principles will be followed by practice suggestions based on decades of experience in supervising the dissertations and theses of graduate students, my studies and practice of art-based research, and a sense of future developments and challenges inside and outside higher education and professions. I offer recommendations for doing and presenting art-based research. Consistent with the one-of-a-kind nature of artistic inquiries, I avoid presenting pre-existing models as emphasized above and offer brief vignettes of exemplary work and future possibilities.

The practical discussion ranges from dealing with compulsory social science research formats in higher education and adapting them to artistic inquiry and presentations, to describing various features of art-based research emerging from my work with doctoral students. For example, new and accessible media have exponentially advanced the creation of art evidence involving physical materials, environments, and action—catalyzing art-based research in ways that parallel historic developments of scientific technology. In the early 1970s, when exploring the use of video in nascent forms of artistic inquiry (McNiff & Cook, 1975), this possibility was suggested, never imagining where we are now with abundant resources readily available and inviting use.

New media, expanding and democratizing the tradition of *cinéma vérité* with spontaneous creations happening on the streets of the world, make it possible to fully realize that art is the evidence generated by art-based research. With accessible and high-quality digital video and photographic technology, we can now document, closely and systematically study, and convincingly present the action of artistic experimentation and its outcomes. Verbal language and concepts, as hopefully shown here, further reflection and communication of artistic processes and their connections to experience but cannot replace direct perception—seeing, hearing, feeling, and examining the physical evidence offered by art-based research.

The methods of artistic inquiry are forever expanding congruent with the process of art. This openness and flexibility can be challenging because many feel the need to follow approved protocols, and thus their predominance in academic and professional research. Art, as discussed here, has a more fluid relationship with rules, prescribed procedures, and uncertainty. The creative tension is good and inspires this effort to make a place for art in research.

Among the issues discussed in the concluding section focused on the future, I address the frequent question regarding who can do art-based research? What kind of background and skills are required? In response, I recommend the most complete inclusion of participants rather than restricting involvement to trained artists, which will limit transdisciplinary cooperation and innovation.

Artistic expression is approached as a universally accessible process and intelligence where people with experience in various backgrounds can make important contributions if they are willing to commit to disciplined and sustained practice. Artistic inquiry will be enriched and deepened by a breadth of participation and imagination. Here, I might mention a quantitative measure and say that my experience working with many thousands of people in studio groups throughout the world repeatedly demonstrates that experienced artists and beginners can work effectively together, influencing and inspiring one another. The principle of open participation is congruent with what I describe as the ecology of creation (2025; 1998b, pp. 11, 20–21), which suggests the interdependence of all life and a more complete vision of research that includes art.

Note

1. Martha Graham affirms this principle in a communication with Agnes de Mille: "There is a vitality, a life force, an energy, a quickening that is translated through you into action, and because there is only one of you in all of time, this expression is unique. And if you block it, it will never exist through any other medium and it will be lost. The world will not have it" (Popova, 2024). For reference, see p. xv.

1

Foundations and Guiding Principles

Original premise and paradigm clarity

My work with students integrating art and therapy during the 1970s and early 1980s led to rethinking assumptions about thesis writing. There was a programmatic and professional expectation that their research would be done in a psychological format, reflecting on how they engaged other people with artistic expression. I assumed the same. Yet my own practice, teaching, and writing were always informed by personal artistic inquiry, and I saw the contradictions between the studio training groups I led and thesis expectations.

My advisees asked questions that were mine as well:

- Why are we required to follow behavioral science research methods and formats for presentation when our discipline is based on the premise that artistic expression offers different ways of discovery, communication, understanding, and healing?
- Is it possible to conduct research that is consistent with the artistic processes we are engaging, and how can I truly know them without becoming directly involved myself?
- Why diminish the impact and clarity of art outcomes, and potentially confuse the research, by translating them into something other than themselves? Doesn't art speak for itself?

They were right. I had to enlarge my views regarding formal and planned academic research and make them more consistent with my convictions about artistic practice. The realization evolved naturally in a process of co-creation with many others.[1] I learned at the start of my career how art-based research was the obvious and most direct way to explore and understand the art experience; how it was congruent with artmaking and naturally extended from it; and how illuminating, accessible, clear, and inspirational it can be.

The graduate students led the way. For example, Catherine Cobb who set out to explore storytelling by young children, informed by Edith Cobb's study of imagination in childhood (1977/1993), began her master's thesis by creating a series of 26 drawings arranged in a pictorial story sequence without text. She then engaged individual children, ages 3½ to 11, and encouraged them to create spontaneous spoken stories in response to the images (Figures 1.1 and 1.2), which were recorded.

Originally trying to distance herself from the children's storytelling in order to study the process with less bias, she

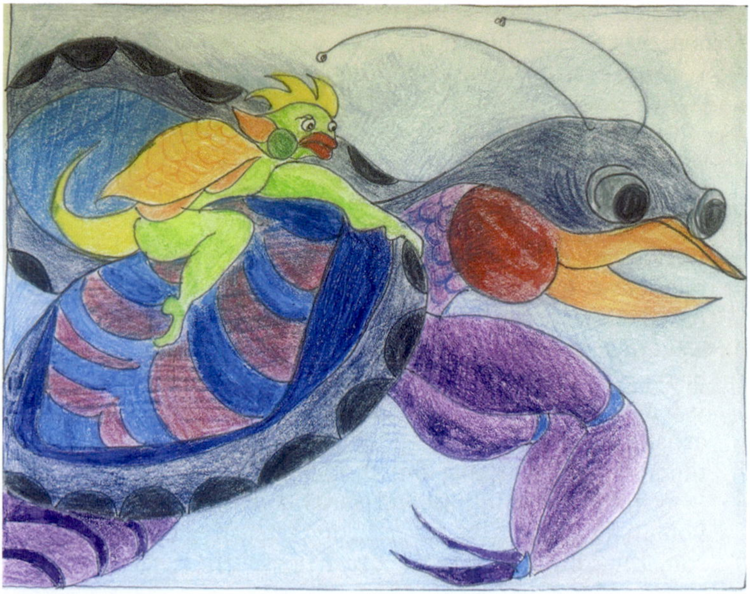

Figure 1.1: Catherine Cobb, *The Rescue*, 1983–1984. Pencil on paper. 6.5 in. × 8 in. © Catherine Cobb.

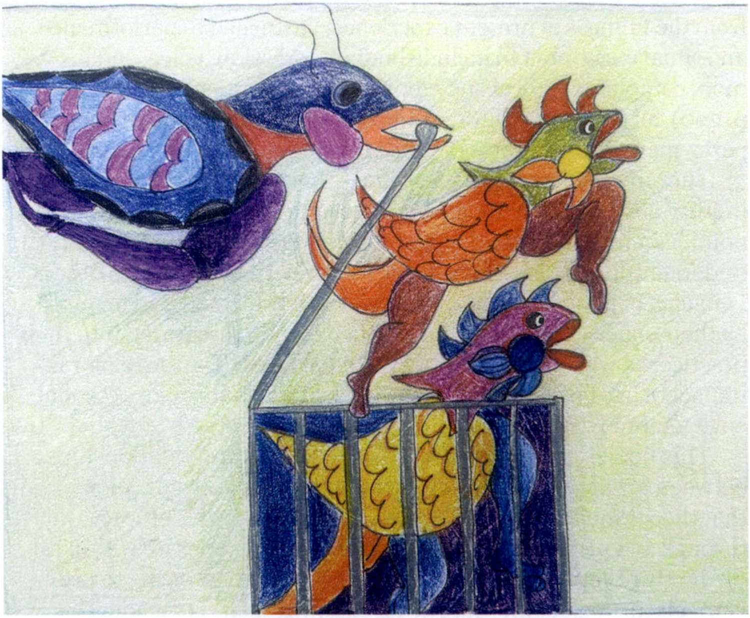

Figure 1.2: Catherine Cobb, *Release of "Creatures,"* 1983–1984. Pencil on paper. 6.5 in. × 8 in. © Catherine Cobb.

describes the unexpected outcome as "a shared creative expression," with the children offering varied imaginative interpretations in a process of reciprocal creation (Cobb, 1984). Over the years, this dimension of co-creation together *with* research partners has characterized art-based research involving other people. It presents a distinct contrast to the conventional social science focus on *subjects*, with as little personal involvement as possible by the person(s) conducting the research.

During this period of the early 1980s, what I later called *art-based research*, had firmly taken hold as the preferred mode of inquiry by the master's theses students I supervised (McNiff, 1986a, 1986b, 1987, 1988). The approach was solidified and affirmed by cooperation with European colleagues, including Louis van Marissing and Klaus Boegel in the Netherlands—the latter describing his 1977–1979 *Tigermann* performance art experimentation as a "form of research" responding to the feeling that his art was "split" from the fullness of present experience. He turned to performance and ritual enactment to include bodily expression, voice, and his more complete physical and emotional environment (McNiff, 1988, p. 220), all of which reinforced my commitment to spontaneous performance art as a form of total art expression.

The "impact factor" of these and other examples of artistic inquiry and the art evidence they present, from my vantage point, can be determined by their influence on my practice and understanding of the issues explored, and, through me, to others I engage, expanding to all people who are informed and inspired by their experience of the work, which is then integrated into their practice, as with the history of art. In terms of the more general impact of art-based research, art evidence acts through personal engagement with it.

This book's emphasis on both distinctions and relationships between art and science responds to the general assumption that the various applied art fields will research their efficacy through scientific methods and metrics, which operate within a distinctly different paradigm—perhaps likened to trying to prove yourself through something other than yourself. I consider this to be a major research disorder and failure to acknowledge the fundamentally different life and reality perspectives on which the disciplines are based, as will be discussed here.

Art and science are complementary, often intertwined, and share many features, but they are different modes of inquiry. Even though there are many different kinds of science and art, neither can be reduced to or justified by the other. Nor do I wish to suggest an all-encompassing art–science duality in relation to research and in any way impede the integral nature of experience and contributions by the multitude of current and future disciplines participating in a truly inclusive community of inquiry. Art welcomes partnerships with all.

What is called art-based research originated and developed within applied art disciplines, which cooperate with mental health, education, medicine, social services, and other professional areas defining their underpinnings as scientific. In my experience, leaders in these fields welcome the contributions of art, respect the expertise of its various disciplines, and distinguish them from science. It is often the applied arts fields themselves that insist on scientific justification as a means of furthering assimilation, recognition, and growth in the respective areas of practice. Regarding art therapy, Pat Allen describes how the fervor to validate itself in this way has produced a "clinification syndrome" which minimizes the medicines of art (1992). Although this dialectal tension is not as dominant within the fine arts community where there is perhaps greater sensitivity to the historical role of art in furthering human understanding and culture, it must similarly deal with governmental, academic, and public assumptions about the nature of research which do not include the making of art (Bast, 2020; Borgdorff, 2012; Frayling, 1993/1994).

Partnerships, interdisciplinary cooperation, and integral relations will be strengthened by supporting and understanding the different paradigms upon which art and science are based, and how they can support a common purpose. The partners are distinct and maintain their integrity, which furthers co-creation, in contrast to the confusion of attempting to know art through science, which can be likened to trying to know one person through another.

In relation to advancing the art process in various fields related to human well-being, I am convinced that attempting to transpose artistic outcomes into scientific formulations obscures them. I have learned to trust and never underestimate the ability of others in various disciplines, especially leaders closely attuned to the needs of the people they serve, to understand and appreciate effective art evidence. This was affirmed recently by Mitchell Kossak's description of its impact on hospital administrators and donors who "see and feel" the work and then support it with funding (2025). I consistently find that the interpretations and questions generated in response to these presentations offer new insights and perspectives that enrich and deepen practice. Expanding the discourse and making it accessible and clear to varied constituents furthers innovation.

Paradigm friction can be viewed as a productive and creative force. This book emanates from it, and arguably the idea and formal discipline of art-based research as well. As I have learned, conflict defines, generating action and change. It is a predictable outcome of innovation and exploring frontiers of practice between disciplines, especially when operating as a relatively small participant making new contributions to large and established spheres. I have learned to embrace conflict and see it as responsible for everything I have done in presenting alternative ways of approaching research and relationships between art and psychology. As with art healing, our difficulties are the sources of their transformation and renewal.

Defining art-based research

I define art-based research as the use of artmaking as the primary mode of inquiry by a person doing the research, alone and/or with others (McNiff, 2013, p. xv). The process trusts artistic intelligence to both explore phenomena in all aspects of life and present discoveries in convincing ways. It is the firsthand artistic inquiry of the persons conducting the research that distinguishes what I call art-based research from often noteworthy studies in various disciplines that reflect upon and examine the artworks and artistic processes of others through more conventional academic structures.

A definition of art-based research invites consideration of the terms *art* and *research*. The latter can be described as a systematic inquiry conducted informally in all of life and formally within various academic and professional disciplines, including art, which, like science, often involves experimentation. In this respect, art and science share many features, each being enhanced through an integral relationship. The concept of art includes all forms of artmaking as emphasized by Susanne K. Langer[2] and is best defined not through explanatory language, which has proven to be inadequate, but by its continuous and tangible creations throughout history—the living and definitive art evidence.

In addition to traditional disciplines of artistic expression, I have always supported the breadth of artistic practice beyond them—the art of teaching, therapy, and other forms of professional and personal practice; scientific investigation to be discussed here in relation to W. I. B. Beveridge; and Otto Rank's advocacy for a new "artist-type" engaging all of life (1968). While recognizing the ongoing contributions of established art forms and their major role in advancing art-based research, I welcome the relaxation of boundaries and a shared perspective of creation, opening to endless new approaches to artmaking.

Rather than attempting to convert artistic processes and outcomes into social science formats, we affirm how *art is the evidence* generated by art-based research; and the quality of the presentation, as with artistic practice, influences impact (McNiff, 2014a, 2014b, 2022). The methods of inquiry, like art, are infinitely variable. Replicability, calculability, and controls under the same conditions are not the goal, nor are they a feature of the endlessly unpredictable nature of artistic processes and the life situations in which they are created. As with artistic expression, we do not attempt to identify general laws,[3] although it is often possible to suggest the presence of consistent forces, tendencies, and effects, as well as generalizable value and usefulness regarding methods and principles of practice, both discovered and perfected by the research. Perhaps it can be said, in the spirit of scientific objectives, that the unpredictable outcomes of the creative process have a certain degree of general predictability.

Art's embrace of personal experience, unpredictability, and emotion can be viewed as unlike science as it is perceived and practiced today, but these defining characteristics in no way suggest anti-science (Holton, 1994). Rather, art-based research is a different mode of inquiry, furthering access to a more complete spectrum of human understanding. In discussing art together with science, it is important to distinguish how the current sense of the latter word, here and in more general discourse, concerns research conducted according to what is now described as "the scientific method," which differs from the Latin *scientia*, knowledge or knowing. The original usage includes artistic understanding and is thus often apt to create confusion.

Nobel Laureate Richard Feynman, who in addition to his contributions to quantum physics practiced painting and percussive music, acknowledged the complementary nature of art and science and gave considerable attention to describing what the latter is and is not. He spoke of how science, like art, "takes a lot of imagination," but in contrast to the infinite range of artistic methods, science operates in a tight-fitting experimental "straitjacket," where ideas are tested and perfected in relation to physical laws. The experiments are then assessed by their believability and the evidence they generate. He felt that copying the forms of science to explain complex human behavior is "pseudo-science" (2025, 1969), an "intellectual tyranny in the name of science."[4] He describes how scientific discovery occurs through experience and gives the example of a young art student realizing the grade differences in the hardness and softness of pencils by using them rather than through verbal definitions. Feynman simply defines science as always questioning and "rechecking" past discoveries and cultural assumptions through "new direct experience" rather than accepting prevailing beliefs (1969).

Art-based research shares the underpinning of discovery through experience with science, but rather than replicating and testing past experiments, each project, while sharing qualities with the more general discipline of artistic inquiry, is distinguished by its singular nature, again in accord with art, which forever makes itself anew. Art is a community of creation where we are influenced by what others have done and then make our own distinctive contributions, as evidenced by the expanding literature describing the broad use of art in research (Barone & Eisner, 2012; Hervey, 2000; Knowles & Cole, 2008; Leavy, 2009, 2018, 2025; Lett, 2016; Liamputtong & Rumbold, 2008; Mateus-Berr & Jochum, 2020; McNiff, 2013; Nash, 2019, 2022; Prior, 2018b; Sullivan, 2004; and many others).

I have always urged students to study what others, including myself, do and advise, but then create their own ways of practice and research. This can be challenging today, when the general assumption is that research dealing with human behavior will follow institutionally sanctioned methods which often involve fixed linear steps—sometimes even thinking the formulaic procedures, with their accompanying ideology and language, are art-based. The resulting work is all too often a repetition and reinforcement of a pre-existing method, or as Hans-George Gadamer said, a production of "regularities" (1994, p. 4). In his novel *The Long Long Way*, Sebastian Barry's character, Mr. Lawler, states the problem clearly—"The curse of the world is people thinking thoughts that are only thoughts which have been given to them. They're not their own thoughts" (2005, p. 9).

In some extreme areas of social science, only "studies" conducted within the permitted formats and paradigm are allowed to be included in reviews of literature and citations, which intensifies the repetition of the same. These strictures, in effect, make classic contributions to academic and professional fields off-limits, especially problematic in psychology, where so many of the formative works do not fit the current mold.

As an artist involved with research, I have a history and approach, which can be examined, just as we study the art of others—perhaps incorporating aspects of their expression into yours and appreciating shared qualities, but never attempting to work exactly as they do. This feature of artistic inquiry not only assures an inclusive community of practice but also keeps research moving and changing into the future.

Needs for structure are real and tend to be universal. When helping others express themselves in various art forms, I emphasize how *structure liberates* when it is grounded in the essential processes of free and personal artistic expression. In affirming the importance of structure in art-based research, the question is—follow and repeat the methods already established by others, or create your own, as artists do?

The idea and practice of art-based research have taken shape within academic settings emphasizing planned inquiry, which might at first seem to contradict how artistic discoveries emanate organically from the often-unexpected dynamics of creating. This book will explore ways of navigating planned and unplanned processes in artistic inquiry. It will also emphasize the persistence and importance of natural art experiments in the world at large—how the idea and formal practice of art-based research has emerged from them, as documented here, and will continue to do so, suggesting the necessity of appreciating and supporting the primacy of free, open, and universally accessible artistic experimentation.

Institutional challenges

> *Paintings are but research and experiment. I never do a painting as a work of art. All of them are researches.*
>
> Pablo Picasso (in Liberman, 1956)

We use the term art-based research (ABR),[5] within the context of "language games" described by Ludwig Wittgenstein (1953), in this case, the academic research "game" with its extensive system of classifications, which now includes art-based research. The name has a practical purpose in establishing a presence within the discourse on the nature of research and different ways of doing it, and the creation of this formal category has led to a certain degree of institutional recognition.

As I will document in the following sections, artistic inquiry has a long and rich history in world cultures. Like so many others, my experience with it emerged intuitively when responding to life experience through artistic expression—while perceiving what I was doing at first as art, not research. In the early 1970s, I innately focused my painting on the people and environments with whom I cooperated in establishing new approaches to art as therapy (Figures 1.3 and 1.4). As I will describe in the forthcoming

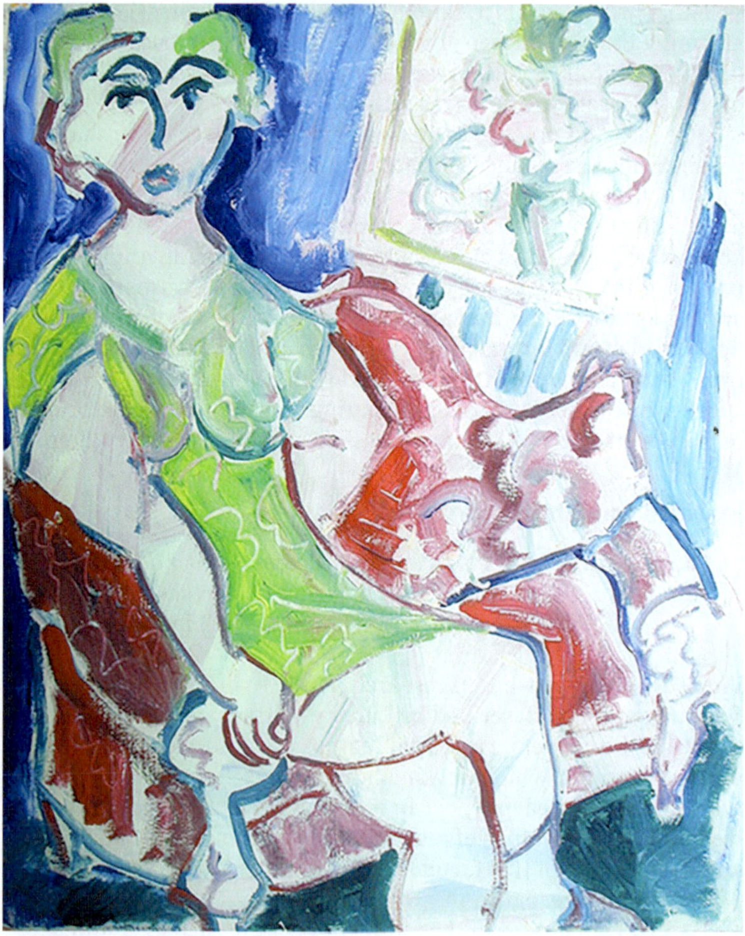

Figure 1.3: Shaun McNiff, *Leah in the Studio*, late 1970s. Acrylic on canvas. 24 in. × 30 in. © Shaun McNiff.

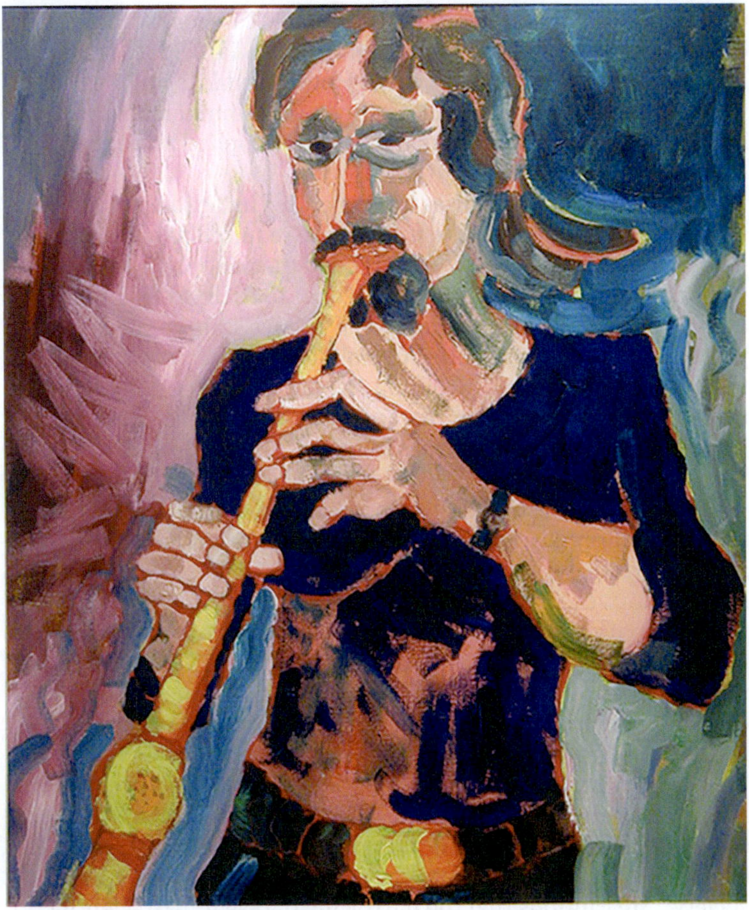

Figure 1.4: Shaun McNiff, *Paolo Knill*, late 1970s. Acrylic on canvas. 30 in. × 36 in. © Shaun McNiff.

pages, the art process progressively evolved into a more systematic use of personal artistic expression to understand and enhance professional practice with others, realizing an integration of art and research.

Ideally, in my view, an integral and truly inclusive concept of research incorporates art together with science and other disciplines and does not require yet another category within the ever-expanding panoply of behavioral and social science research types and the divisions they create. However, this is not the case with research today, especially in the realm of human behavior, health, education, and related areas, where applied art practice occurs.

Proliferation of categories has generated an academic industry within social science, where students are required to take courses designed to enable them to comprehend the panoply. The maze of research types bears little resemblance to Richard Feynman's emphasis on how the physical laws of science state complex processes simply (1967). Most troubling is the dominant attitude that human experience, including art, can only be understood through science, a position that Ray Monk (1999) feels results in ponderous language and flawed theorizing that would make Wittgenstein weep.

There has been support and longstanding initiatives with the fine arts community for the idea of art as research (Borgdorff, 2012; Frayling, 1993/1994; Mateus-Berr & Jochum, 2020; Nelson, 2013; Prior, 2012), where artistic inquiry often takes place more naturally with artists doing *research* with various art forms. But if sustaining the polymath legacy of Leonardo Da Vinci by dealing with social, health, scientific, and environmental questions in cooperation with other disciplines, professional artistic training will confront paradigm conflicts discussed here.

Gerald Bast, President Emeritus of the University of Applied Arts Vienna, describes how the prevailing assumption that art "can only be an object of (scientific) research"[6] overlooks historical evidence of art's contributions to "understanding and shaping society." He cautions that the narrowing of research to scientific methods contradicts the ever-increasing complexity of experience and limits our ability to deal with it (2020, p. 2).

This is the landscape in which research concerning human experience currently takes place. The whole process can be viewed as an unplanned and extended natural experiment documenting the divisive tendencies of human systems. Within the quantitative–qualitative bifurcation of behavioral and social science, art-based research is often included today in the latter category. This is in some ways a positive development, furthering access, but the classification potentially ties artistic inquiry to the language, formats, silos, and research expectations of what can be viewed as an incompatible paradigm. Therefore, we cannot definitely say that art-based research is qualitative research. I have never described it this way. Aside from the fact that certain forms of artmaking might sometimes have a distinctly quantitative aspect, the scientized schema limits artistic inquiry, which—as we are seeing from its worldwide growth—can contribute to various academic and professional areas.

Also, as I emphasize in this book, artworks are empirical phenomena, even temporal artistic expressions generated in moments of time, and do not completely align with the core premise of "qualia" as internal mental states connected to how we experience and feel the world distinct from the physical things and life forms we perceive.

Art and science share essential features—disciplined and systematic inquiry, precise observation and understanding of phenomena, experimentation, creation of knowledge, problem-solving, imagination, curiosity, commitments to quality and life-enhancing innovation, respect for the contributions of accidents and mistakes, effective communication, empirical methods and outcomes, and more. The professional and corporate forms of both domains have simply generated separations that do not exist at the basis of natural learning, creating, and inquiry in varied life situations. On a practical basis in daily life, now and for millennia, art–science integration happens naturally.

When I began to work with art and mental health in 1970, the integration of artistic processes and psychology was relatively unrestricted. Artists and psychologists were committed to developing shared language and conversation. Because the professional practice of art therapy was nascent, I could fluidity join psychology and art which aligned closely with the work I was doing and this was affirmed by many within the psychological community, like Pat Musick (2024) and her psychology colleagues at Cornell University inviting me to participate in their symposium on Psychology and the Artistic Process at the American Psychological Association Annual Convention (McNiff, 1975b). Art-based research emerged from these pragmatic efforts to understand and perfect practice through experimentation and reflection. There was full access to art, psychology, philosophy, medicine, history, religion, and all disciplines and traditions furthering understanding of current practice, and especially the historic cross-cultural continuities of art healing (McNiff, 1979).

A study examining the rise of what is called qualitative research describes how it did not exist outside the phenomenological school of philosophy in its initial years. It took shape within psychology in the 1980s and grew rapidly in the 1990s (Rennie et al., 2002), a period Frederick Wertz auspiciously describes as a "revolutionary institutionalization of qualitative methods" (2014, p. 4). It is important to emphasize that this happened well after the initial work we did with artistic inquiry. The dualistic quantitative–qualitative language, and the eventual scientization of all institutional psychology and the format dominance emerging from it to be discussed here,[7] were not an issue in the formative years of art-based research.

The rapid development and assimilation of the qualitative concept, consolidating the spectrum of "non-quantitative research," presented psychology exclusively as science rather than recognizing the different modes of inquiry for what they are and acknowledging how psychologizing, in the words of Walt Whitman "contains multitudes"—in this case beyond the quantitative–qualitative limits. Ironically, not only did the "qualitative" perspective take shape recently in philosophy, but all of psychology emerged from earlier philosophical foundations.

In its efforts to cast itself exclusively as science, psychology—one of the most active interdisciplinary partners with art—denies its deep-seated origins in the humanities and is unable to engage all of Psyche. Eugene O'Neill reminded the world that: "Authors were psychologists ... before psychology was invented" (Bogard & Bryer, 1994, p. 386). As I emphasize here, what we now call art-based research is not new and has a rich legacy in literature and other art forms.

The absence of shared conceptual foundations and the questionable relevance of natural science methods and formats to every area of inquiry undermine an integral psychological identity (Uher, 2021; Zagaria et al., 2020). Consequently, much done in the name of science is far from it. The never-ending classifications of research, especially in the so-called qualitative sector, can be viewed as a manifestation of psychology seeking its completeness within a system of typologies that will never contain the infinite uniqueness and complexity of persons, experience, and creation.

Even within art-based research, an expansive list of categories and fixed methods, too many to mention here, continuously emerge and threaten the unity of purpose, together with a division of art forms corresponding to academic and professional structures. Ross W. Prior, founding and principal editor of the *Journal of Applied Arts & Health*, has expressed concern about fragmentation of effort—"The separations reinforce the current lack of integral vision, rather than strengthening the whole community, history and future potential of art and artistic understanding to reinforce a common purpose" (2018b, p. xviii).

Research, in the complete sense of the concept, prominently includes science but is not restricted to it. As much as I would like research to be reclaimed as all-inclusive and embracing varied modes of inquiry, institutional departmentalization, and its ever-increasing specializations with different principles of faith (McNiff, 1986a) make this unlikely today. The physicist Gerald Holton describes how underlying belief systems as to the nature of life, the *Weltbild* of a particular era not unlike organized religion, determine what kinds of research are supported (1994, pp. 157–159). Therefore, an epistemological case must be made for research through art within academic and professional institutions together with providing convincing presentations of experimentation and outcomes. In this era, when many feel that justification can be realized only through science, there is a need for "full confidence," as Ross W. Prior encourages, in art as a source of "knowing and being" (Angelopoulo et al., in press).

While sympathizing with those within psychology encouraging an integrative identity affirming the pluralism of the discipline, I feel that this can be done only by acknowledging the breadth and depth of psychological practice as both art and science. The exclusive identification of psychology, and its focus on human understanding, with the realm of social science is questionable.

Free movement of ideas and research

Rudolf Arnheim was the seminal figure in developing the psychology of art, and he did this in a manner that keeps "the smell of the studio" (1974, p. 4). In a letter to me in response to the publication of *Art-Based Research*, he emphasized the importance of "keeping the concepts of art and science free from the usual restrictive definitions":

> Every piece of artwork, even the simplest, deserves to be called art when its form carries the expression of a genuine human experience and science is not limited to measurement and statistic, but includes any systematic investigation of a fact of life and nature, even when a child explores the inside of a pinecone or an egg.
>
> (Arnheim, 1998)

Together with Arnheim and many others throughout history, I affirm cooperation between art and science and an appreciation of their shared qualities and purpose in understanding and enhancing experience. Arnheim's definition clearly integrates art and science, an issue I will explore in the concluding section of this book. But the partnership currently requires considerable change.

Where science is largely perceived as examining life with the goal of testing hypotheses to generate theories and laws of nature, art offers the uniqueness of individual and collective creations enriching life. Again, they are complementary disciplines, each with longstanding traditions and comprehensive communities of practice. Science generally strives to be impersonal, consistent, and predictable—art does not. Both have transcendent dimensions, but art is linked to the artists who make it, as I will discuss in the following section. Science describes itself as using systematic methods of experimentation generating evidence, and I will show that the same applies to art. In this respect, there is considerable misunderstanding as to the nature of the disciplines, their relationship with one another, and historical cooperation in psychology and other fields. Art and science have become thoroughly departmentalized, an institutional rather than epistemological reality that I accept as a basis for this text, whose purpose is to address the silos of contemporary academic and professional systems and make a place for research through art.

During his years as professor of the psychology of art at Harvard, Arnheim overlapped with the prominent behavioral psychologist B. F. Skinner, known as the penultimate laboratory scientist advocating a controversial "technology of behavior" (1971), which rejects consciousness and inner motivations while establishing the dominance of scientific psychology in the United States. He makes important contributions to understanding how environments and reinforcement influence behavior, but I see this principle as part of a larger interplay of factors and not an exclusive determinant.

Skinner, who studied literature and aspired to be a writer as an undergraduate, may have written his most compelling exegesis of operant conditioning in *Walden Two* (1968), an undeclared and ironic masterwork of art-based research which "reinforces" this book's emphasis on the breadth of possibilities characterizing artistic inquiry. The novel opens with Rogers, a recent World War II veteran visiting the protagonist, his former professor, Burris.

In their conversation, Rogers challenges the assumption that answers to social problems are generated by academic research:

> It's a job for research, but not the kind you can do in a university, or in a laboratory anywhere. I mean you've got to experiment, and *experiment with your own life!* Not just sit back—not just sit back in an ivory tower somewhere—as if your own life weren't all mixed up in it.
>
> (1968, p. 9, original emphasis)

Skinner's "many-sided" life corresponds to the complex of art, psychology, science, and their mixings with experience and the contradictions that we see today. For example, his "A Lecture on 'Having' a Poem" (1972), given at the Poetry Center in New York City in 1971, presents a distinctively Skinnerian and engaging reflection on the making of art, which describes poems emerging through the poet in ways that correspond to childbirth—I have similarly likened artistic expressions to offspring, closely related to their creators but unquestionably independent entities (2004, p. 90).

Skinner proposes that poets operate in a specific place and time, shaped by genetic and environmental influences together with their personal histories, including what has been learned through experience, the effects of previous efforts, and a more general process of reinforcement. By studying these processes, he believes we can become more effective in making poems, and other art forms, and ultimately create environments that support their realization. In response, and based on my experience and work with helping others, I say yes, to all these points, which enrich the larger inquiry into the nature of artmaking. They certainly make more sense than psychodynamic reductions of artistic expressions to early childhood sexual factors. I believe that effective teachers and others supporting artistic expression in society would concur.

My questions, if I could present them to the esteemed psychologist and writer who might possibly be open to this book's focus on concrete and observable art evidence, are: Did these insights and recommendations take shape through your experience with creative writing? Through your "own life," or in "a laboratory anywhere"? Through a mix of them all?

I believe his reliable ideas and practices can contribute to a larger and open discourse as to the nature of artmaking, which also includes memory and imagination, spontaneous acts, chance influences, visions and aspirations, and other elements that are not necessarily subject to controlled conditions.

In relation to this book's emphasis on the one-of-a-kind qualities of art-based research, Burrhus Frederic Skinner is a psychologist-artist, or artist-psychologist, like no other. He has been described as leading a "double life" (Baars, 2003) but this attribution, although accurate in perhaps describing different aspects of his psychological and artistic life, proposes a split condition. I see B. F. Skinner manifesting his "manyness," what James Hillman describes as the fundamental multiplicity of persons and life to be kept "from dominion by any singular power" (1977, p. 32).

Moving beyond the sphere of individual persons and considering the broader existence of ideas sans "the usual restrictive definitions," art, science, and everything else can be approached as partaking in an ecology of creation, the depth and vitality of which depends upon the quality and imagination of the participating elements.

Good ideas will always cross over the enclosures we construct and create new life. The boundaries, restrictions, and controlling powers of institutions, professions, and the identities extending from them can be relaxed to encourage the free movement of ideas and research, in keeping with the realities of nature.

Notes

1. When I subsequently read Elliot Eisner's work dealing with "artistic approaches to qualitative research" (1981, 1997), leading

to what he later called "arts-based educational research," ABER (Barone & Eisner, 1997, 2006), I imagined him experiencing a similar process in his interactions with art education graduate students. Core elements of research and understanding through art transcend any one person's engagement with them at particular moments of time. The same applies to the terms we use to describe the process, which can limit possibilities. As important as descriptive language is in making a place for artistic inquiry within the broader context of research, I encourage the most inclusive and fluid definitions. For reference, see p. 2.

2. "It is in pursuing the differences among them [art forms] that one arrives, finally, at a point where no more differences appear; then one has found, not postulated, their unity. At that deep level there is only one concept exemplified in all the different arts, and that is the concept of Art" (Langer, 1957, p. 14). See p. 6.
3. Something that Alasdair MacIntyre feels has not been accomplished by social science due to the unpredictability of human behavior. He encourages the various disciplines dealing with human experience to focus on *phronesis*, practical wisdom (2007). Neil Postman, like MacIntyre, insists that the social sciences have not identified "immutable" laws, and while affirming their importance he believes they, and other areas dealing with human creations, "do not do science" (1984, p. 23). See p. 7.
4. The United Kingdom Science Council announced in 2009 that it spent a year developing "a definition of science," claiming it to be the first official definition to be published: "Science is the pursuit of knowledge and understanding of the natural and social world following a systematic methodology based on evidence" (2025). The explanation lacks empirical specificity regarding method and evidence and sustains the uniform application of allegedly scientific forms to all of human experience. I do not think Richard Feynman would like it (https://sciencecouncil.org/about-science/our-definition-of-science/). See p. 7.
5. The acronym has served a practical purpose, but I prefer non-technical, directly descriptive, and jargon-free language, such as artistic inquiry, art as research, artistic research, research through art, all in sync with the discipline of art-based research. ABR can also create confusion since it is widespread in different professional and business areas. The increasing use of acronyms in the current era limits inclusive discourse, since many are not familiar with them. See p. 9.

6. Bast's position concurs with Ross W. Prior's assertion that art can be the "topic, process and outcome" of research (2018a, pp. 45–60). See p. 12.
7. Scientism can be defined as the belief that the methods of natural science are to be applied to all research as the only true sources of understanding. It will inevitably generate pseudo-science as Richard Feynman emphasizes, diluting science and obfuscating other disciplines. Although I do not share her focus on the various "post" and "de" ideologies prevalent today, a discussion beyond my purpose here, I want to acknowledge how the critique of qualitative research developed by Elizabeth Adams St. Pierre (2021) appears to be in total sync with this book's criticism of prescriptive and fixed research methods and their standardizations. This coincidence perhaps offers yet another natural experiment, affirming how similar practical approaches to the research process and deeply held convictions can emerge and converge from distinctly different vantage points and research content, arguably a significant and yet another unplanned outcome. See p. 14.

2

Personal and Empirical: A Pervasive Misunderstanding

> *The expressive urge can be understood only as an ever-present atmosphere .... For that reason one cannot convince anyone of its existence who has not ... experienced it directly, and we shall not discuss it further but turn instead to the pictures in which it is evident.*
>
> Hans Prinzhorn (1972, p. 14, original publication 1922)

Embracing and transcending the personal

In addition to restrictive assumptions about art's relationship to research, there is a general perception that it is exclusively a mode of personal expression. This, together with other limiting concepts with historic antecedents, has deterred appreciation of art as a source of knowledge and understanding. While affirming the personal nature of artistic expressions, it can be asked whether they also manifest shared human and natural processes? Do they embrace and transcend the personal?

In this discussion, transcendence is approached pragmatically and does not suggest supernatural phenomena. Thomas Berry preferred the word "*inscendence*," opening to the genetic sources of life (2015, pp. 207–208) to guide present experience. I see the two terms as complementary, with both emphasizing how personal actions can have significance beyond themselves.

The tendency to dismiss art-based research as mere personal introspection is bolstered by the belief that knowledge is exclusively generated through more impersonal rational thought grounded in linear-logical processes. Reason is affirmed here, but not considered the only source of human understanding, which is much larger and more inclusive.

Those who insist that the discipline of art therapy must justify itself through something other than art itself might consider how the term and concept of *art therapy* emerged through Adrian Hill's use of personal artistic expression to further recovery from tuberculosis when confined to a sanitorium bed in 1938 (1945). Having served in the British Army during World War I, his firsthand experience with art healing inspired him to bring it to hospitalized soldiers returning from World War II and to more general health systems in cooperation with the British Red Cross Society.

What is now called art-based research is, as I have mentioned above, innate to what artists have done throughout history. It can present itself as sustaining and renewing what Edvard Munch describes as the artist's use of personal inquiry to understand "what is the universal in the soul": "[I]t is not to describe my own life. I am writing a study of the soul as I observe myself closely and use myself as an anatomical testing-ground" (Munch, 2024).

The fact that artistic expression, albeit personal, is also a thoroughly empirical process, generally with unique physical outcomes, can be viewed as fundamental to understanding art-based research. Where the usual notion of empirical research involves the *direct observation* of experience and life processes, artistic inquiry adds the dimension of personal expression as an exploratory "testing ground." The actions of the persons conducting the research are integral to the overall inquiry and they generate empirical *art evidence*.

Also in the visual arts, Josef Albers initiated what can be viewed as one of the most systematic and sustained empirical research projects in any artistic discipline from 1950 to 1958, when he chaired the Department of Design at the Yale School of Art, building on his experience at Black Mountain College (1933–1949). Through continuous experimentation involving students in his classes, Albers demonstrated the relativity of the visual perception of color, how it is reliably interdependent with its surrounding environment: "[W]e almost never (that is, without special devices) see a single color unconnected and unrelated to other colors. Colors present themselves in continuous flux, constantly related to changing neighbors and changing conditions" (Albers, 1971, p. 5).

This experimentation suggests extensive possibilities for future inquiry in our contemporary ecological era, and its affirmation of the whole and interrelated context of perception aligns closely with the work of Rudolf Arnheim[1] and Kurt Lewin to be discussed here. Where Albers was restricted in the original 1963 publication of *Interaction of Color* by the high cost of color plates and the physical weight of the edition, the presentation of current research is furthered by accessible and high-quality digital media, as I will describe.

Two points of importance regarding the experimentation of Albers in relation to this book are: his emphasis on the "search" process involving new exploration through artistic practice versus "re-search," defined literally as the replication of past experiments (McDonald, 2025); and the distinction of empirical artistic inquiries from what he called "so-called self-expression" (Albers, 1971, p. xiv).

The suggestion that art-based research is purely personal has been reinforced by various factors. Many projects and presentations involving artistic inquiry have been largely and intentionally self-referential, placing less emphasis on also looking beyond the person doing the research. And within the context of behavioral and social science research methods, art-based research is often considered to be a form of what is now called heuristic inquiry and defined as self-investigation, which I consider to be a misuse of the heuristic method—*to discover through experimentation and practical experience,* which closely aligns with artistic inquiry and more general practitioner research. And more recently, the growing tendency within the qualitative sector to describe an examination of personal experience, including artistic inquiry, as "auto-ethnography," designates the studies as ethnographic, or as Wittgenstein might say, framing it all within the behavioral and social science *language game.*

Art-based research, consistent with the history of art, is distinguished by processes and outcomes that exist with a certain degree of autonomy or independence from the ego-spheres of the people who make them. Even if the artistic expression, such as the concept of creating one's own life, as practiced within the Confucian discipline of self-cultivation (McNiff, 2018b; Wei-Ming, 1993), does not result in a physical form distinct from the artist, the primary focus may not be egocentric but rather committed to the broader human community. The process can be likened to the poet Charles Olson saying: Make "traceries sufficient to/other's needs" (1951, p. 53).

In summary, art-based research is viewed here as a mode of disciplined and systematic inquiry that both embraces and transcends the personal features of artistic expression. It is an empirical and experimental process that generates art evidence, which although closely related to the artists creating it and their life experiences, also exists independently from them. And the relevance of the research is generally determined by the extent to which it is useful to others as well as the people who conduct it. Does it further the effectiveness of the practice and understanding of it?

In contrast to science, the art-based research standard of *generalizability* is not assessed by statistical sampling or replication studies. Rather we ask, as with the determination of artistic value, does the research interest and influence others? Does it improve practice? Does it persist into the future, inspire, and further understanding?

Note

1. In acknowledging the contributions of Albers to understanding the contrasting relationships of colors, Arnheim describes how more attention can be given to the "countereffect" of assimilation occurring when colors are similar or the areas holding them are small (1974, p. 364). For reference, see p. 23.

3
A Natural Emanation From Practice

To further this book's focus on practice, I will reflect on how my understanding of art-based research has taken shape incrementally within a larger context of sustained artistic and natural experimentation. Since there was no established tradition or discipline involving the use of artistic expression as research in the areas where I began my work in 1970, my approach to artistic inquiry developed intuitively before crystallizing as a way of doing research. In retrospect, the open-ended and solitary context had many positive implications.

The absence of precedent meant there were no stock methods nor authoritative principles to limit possibilities regarding art as research, which is fundamental to the approach I recommend here—encouraging the distinct artfulness of each research project.

There are two primary and interrelated threads to the following discussion—one dealing with perfecting specific methods of artistic practice with others, which have also been the orientation of much of the doctoral research I have supervised, and the other investigating broader questions regarding the nature of artistic expression with a sustained focus on how art heals.

As I emphasize throughout this book, my personal perspectives on artistic inquiry were formed within this context but I see the discipline of art-based research as transcending them with unlimited future applications. I look forward to new contributions and learning from them.

Formative processes—Liberating artistic interpretation

From the beginning of my involvement with using art to further well-being and human understanding, approaches to practice developed in response to my own experience with artistic expression and reflection on what people did in the state hospital art therapy studio sessions I led. I systematically documented and examined individual and group sessions, archived artworks, immersed myself in the literature related to art and mental health, published the work, and presented it at professional meetings inside and outside the hospital community. I also studied what artists in various disciplines said and wrote about their experience as creators and credit my undergraduate experience with a broad liberal education as seminal.

As a student of the philosophy of art in the 1960s, Susanne K. Langer (1951) and Ernst Cassirer (1975) reinforced my sense that the various forms of artistic expression not only contribute to knowledge but also to understanding the depths of experience. As a Jesuit mentor said to me—reason is a powerful tool, but it can only go so far. In my later work exploring the relationship between art and psychology with Rudolf Arnheim (1972, 1974), I resonated with Hans Prinzhorn's emphasis on "the need for the expression of the psyche ... the expressive urge" existing as a primary motivating force for the creative process with its endlessly different "individual traits" and cultural manifestations (1972, pp. 11–13). I came to both Arnheim and Prinzhorn through art therapy, where I consistently observed the close correspondence between what I empirically observed in a state hospital studio and my own art. Arnheim, who read selections from the original 1922 German publication of Prinzhorn's *Bildnerei der Geisteskranken* to me before it was published in English, demonstrated the principle by putting a finger on his wrist as an expression of our common pulse.

My early writings were striving to support the psychology of art, which has had a mixed history in relation to artistic expression. Rather than using artistic processes to generate "data" to be "analyzed" and reduced to questionable psychological concepts, I was urging psychology, together with art's various applied disciplines in mental health and education, to realize how artistic expressions and artists can deepen and enrich psychological understanding as they have throughout history. I proposed the creation of *an artistic psychology* encouraging a more integral partnership between disciplines, approaching *art as psychological inquiry* (McNiff, 1981a, 1986b).

These commitments have not been abated, and they have been furthered by the *art-based* processes described here.

Cooperation with psychology, and more specifically depth psychology, continues, but as with dance partners, why not let art lead occasionally, or participate equally, rather than always follow.

Together with this mutual relationship between art and psychology, my work has been shaped by calling attention to the misuse of art by various pseudo-science systems and ideologies. When first introduced to art and mental health, I was appalled by how a person's art, especially with visual media, which are more likely to invite projection, was used diagnostically with the belief that the expressions, especially those of a spontaneous nature, reveal psychopathology. People living with emotional difficulties were especially vulnerable to these practices, which often negatively interpret positive artistic expressions—for example, attributing the use of numerous forms to a fragmented psyche. Ironically, in relation to this book's focus on art as evidence, these diagnostic claims that art "unconsciously" and reliably manifests pathological conditions present evidence of diagnosticians projecting their viewpoints and analytic systems onto a person's art.

The psychological assertions were grounded, once again, in the notion that artistic expression is exclusively a form of personal disclosure and that the "psychopathology of expression" will be revealed through art. The bizarre practices are still active today. They are largely associated with psychodynamic theories reducing present behavior, including the life-affirming expressions of art and creative imagination, to various negative and authoritative classifications and judgments usually tied to childhood psychosexual conflicts. Georgia O'Keeffe stated the situation best in response to those who ascribed a relationship between her paintings of flowers and female genitalia—"When people read erotic symbols into my paintings they're really talking about their own affairs" (Saltz, 2023).

The work I was doing with others, and my own art practice, affirmed that an artistic expression, like a person, cannot be reduced to a concept nor label, and especially not by someone other than the one who made it. Our experience consistently confirms that an artwork generates multiple and potentially limitless interpretations, all of which affirm art's ability to transmit expression, foster creative relationships with others, and continuously create new life in the responses to it.

The empirical and open-ended way I perceive a person's artistic expressions is best stated by Shakespeare's *Hamlet* in Act 1, Scene

5—"*There are more things in Heaven and Earth, Horatio, than are dreamt of in your philosophy*" (author's emphasis). Their protean nature cannot be caught by a pre-existing conceptual framework. I have found it more effective to approach artworks and the artists who make them with an attitude of respect, curiosity, and wonder doing my best to open to the inimitability of the present moment. In my teaching and personal practice, I encourage relaxation of the inevitable judgments and realizing the discipline of presence, concentration, and receptivity to the qualities of the artistic expression and its impact on us.

The more I explored my own art in an ongoing and informal process of inquiry, the more I appreciated how my relationship to it continuously changed and elicited different responses, a process which can be viewed as an extended and unplanned natural experiment. Even as a maker of art, my ensuing comments, and descriptions, although informed by the actual creation of the work and its abiding form, are reflections influenced by successive moments in time.

Rather than assuming that an artistic expression is to be described by a single attribution of meaning, I saw how interpretation can be re-visioned as a personal and creative response to an artwork within an ongoing relationship, which is yet another aspect of how art heals in making life anew. Our responses keep renewing artistic expressions and the process does the same for us.

I admire Susan Sontag's classic *Against Interpretation*, which contests *a certain kind of interpretation*—the designation of meanings to artistic expressions based on what is deemed to exist "behind" what they present according to a conceptual "code" (1966, pp. 5–6). Her description of the problem is consistent with my criticism of psychological interpretation and labeling according to a set of authoritative and circumscribed concepts.[1]

The title of Sontag's work suggests categorical opposition to interpretation, which is modified in the essay by a statement that she is not against the fundamental process. Rather, she encourages doing it with greater acuity. Misuse of interpretation results in many feeling that it is inherently bad. Rather than rejecting interpretation, we can do it more artistically and accurately.

Depth is on the surface of artistic expression (McNiff, 2014c, 2015) and the challenge is one of responding to it with greater appreciation, perspicacity, and imagination. Interpretation is essential to our existence. We naturally interpret our environments and life situations as we interact with them through an integration of perception, imagination, and thought. Artists constantly respond to nature and life events through their interpretations. They sometimes also respond to the works of others, creating new renditions in all art forms, perhaps best illustrated by those described as music interpreters. Interpretation is a life-giving process that expands and responds to art with art.

Misguided psychological thinking has furthered my longstanding commitment to advancing a more credible and imaginative view of interpretation. The problem of projecting hidden or symbolic meanings onto a person's expression stems from the ingrained "What does it mean?" response to art. The assumption that only experts can address the question has generated a condition that I call *explanationism*—explaining and reducing artistic expressions to static concepts, rather than simply engaging them as we would another person, opening to relationship and varied conversations over time.

The analytic reduction of artistic expression to something other than itself persists today in social and behavioral science research. If art-based research is to realize its considerable potential, it must distance itself from these constraints and align itself with interpretive processes congruent with artistic experience.

Learning by not doing: A paradoxical realization

In my doctoral research during the mid-1970s, I concentrated on motivation in art. I interviewed artists from various disciplines and spoke with young children about why they made art, with the goal of consciously articulating motives in contrast to the prevailing assumption that artistic expression was an extension of nonconscious and negative psychodynamic contents, generally identified by someone other than the person making the art as described above. The doctorate was awarded in the psychology of art and the research, suggesting a broad and fluid range of consciously accessible motives, was widely presented (McNiff, 1975b, 1977, 1981a).

In relation to my practice of art-based research, the study was significant, ironically, for what I did not do. I was relatively new to the psychology of art and hoping to contribute to it within the *accepted* research discourse. In retrospect, the doctoral work might be considered art-based, since I was conversing freely with artists and children about their involvement in the art process, and much of the text was written in a way that was closer to literary nonfiction dialogue than an academic treatise. And the fundamental challenge to the reduction of life-affirming artworks to unsubstantiated psychodynamic theories was grounded in my experience making art and helping others with their artistic expression.

But I was not dealing directly with the issues of motivation in my own art in the doctoral work, an engagement that in my opinion defines art-based research. As I neared the completion of the doctoral process, my advisor, Van Richards, wanted to know my experience with the issues being explored, frankly asking, How about you? How does this relate to your art?

Since the final draft was complete and approved by the committee, we discussed exhibiting my paintings as a companion to the written text. The idea was strongly supported by the committee, and the paintings, many of which responded to the art and presence of people in the hospital art therapy studio, generated considerable curiosity and discussion in our final meeting held in the exhibit space.

Today, I can appreciate how an in-depth reflection on my own art motives could have enhanced the study in many ways. First, by palpably and transparently showing how, despite the best efforts to minimize bias, the overall process of the research and the person doing it will influence outcomes. It "arguably contradicts the nature of reality" to think we can completely "bracket" our presence and avoid the influence of our thoughts and actions on the issues being examined (McNiff, 2018a, p. 88).

I can also envision how my artistic participation would provide the basis for critical comparison and questioning of the various motives described by others—how my experience may have differed and/or aligned with theirs; how they might have made me aware of dimensions previously overlooked, challenged my assumptions, and affirmed the existence of multiple perspectives and motivations.[2]

And by showing the art evidence and the making of it through video, readers might more completely experience the process and be invited to offer their contributions to the ongoing inquiry. Perhaps most importantly, the reflection on my art, together with the art made by people in the studios I coordinated at the time, would establish a professional precedent for acknowledging and affirming the reality of their interdependent relationship, which as I will show was later demonstrated.

My initial reaction to showing my art was that it made sense in terms of presenting the whole of my work over the course of doctoral study. But I did not think the research *should be about me*. Since I took this position regarding my own work, it offers a firsthand opportunity to explore the issue of personal artistic expression in art-based research.

As my thoughts about art-based research progressed and took shape, I realized that a personal inquiry into my motives and art activity is not necessarily *about me*. To transcend the personal and be useful to others, it must explore the empirical art process in which I am engaged—the materials, the emerging gestures, forms, compositions, and their possible relationships to things, places, people, and experiences outside of myself, and so forth.

Art forms and the process of creation are closely connected to the persons who make them, but also exist autonomously. In terms of egocentrism and self-absorption, it can be said that this applies to the assumption that these distinctly "other" aspects of artistic creation are all part of the artist doing the work. As I have discovered, we are never truly alone when creating but always acting and reflecting together with the world (McNiff, 2015). Thus, an inquiry into the possible motives for my artmaking can involve me in relating to processes and elements beyond me, just as I would do in interviewing another person. In both cases, I am a participant in a relationship that is more than me.

I have not written an autobiography, but having made many paintings and drawings in the genre of self-portraiture in a continuous process that can be viewed as one of many unplanned and extended natural experiments, I consistently discover that despite trying to capture a sense of likeness, albeit in ways more focused on the expressive qualities of gestures and the medium than a facsimile, the outcomes can reliably be called *me and not me*. The same applies to more literal representational paintings and photographic media where, in all cases, the materials and resulting forms, as Arnheim showed, manifest their own, inherent expression, which is "embedded" in their physical form and structure (1974, pp. 449–452).

The art holds qualities of the person making it. When I respond to a landscape, object, or another person, even when working with pure gesture, form, color, and shape, the expressions carry my artistic DNA or style. But when making my best effort to paint a *self-portrait,* I create something materially new, autonomous, maybe related to me in various ways but categorically not me. I have found that the paintings are more effective when I relax the literal notion of likeness and approach the expressive and material qualities as perhaps more authentic portrayals of the person making the art and concentrate more on making the picture and what *it needs* to hopefully realize its expressive potential (Figures 3.1 and 3.2).

The idea and process of "self-portraiture" offer manifold possibilities for art-based research addressing the notion of the self. Is there a fixed and permanent personal identity, or is this concept an illusion as suggested by Eastern traditions?; and as

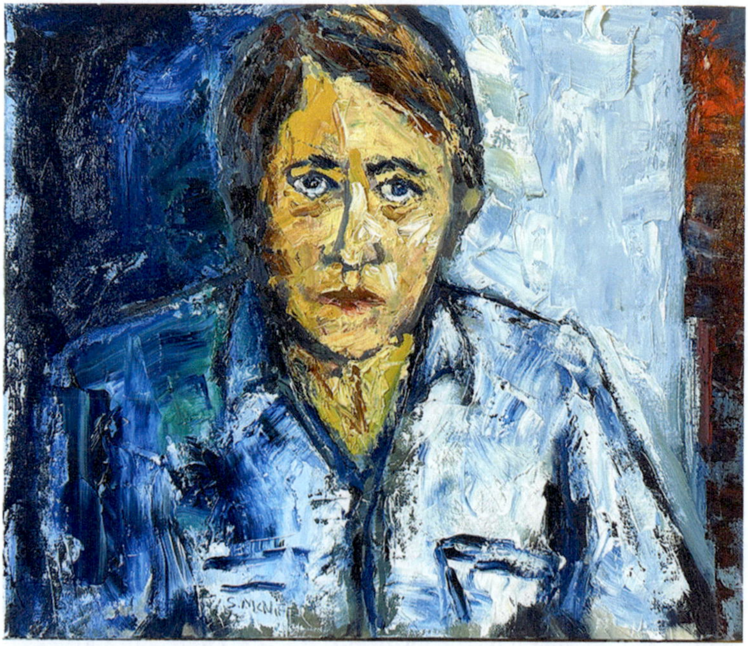

Figure 3.1: Shaun McNiff, *Me & Not Me Impasto,* 2024. Oil on canvas. 20 in. × 23 in. © Shaun McNiff.

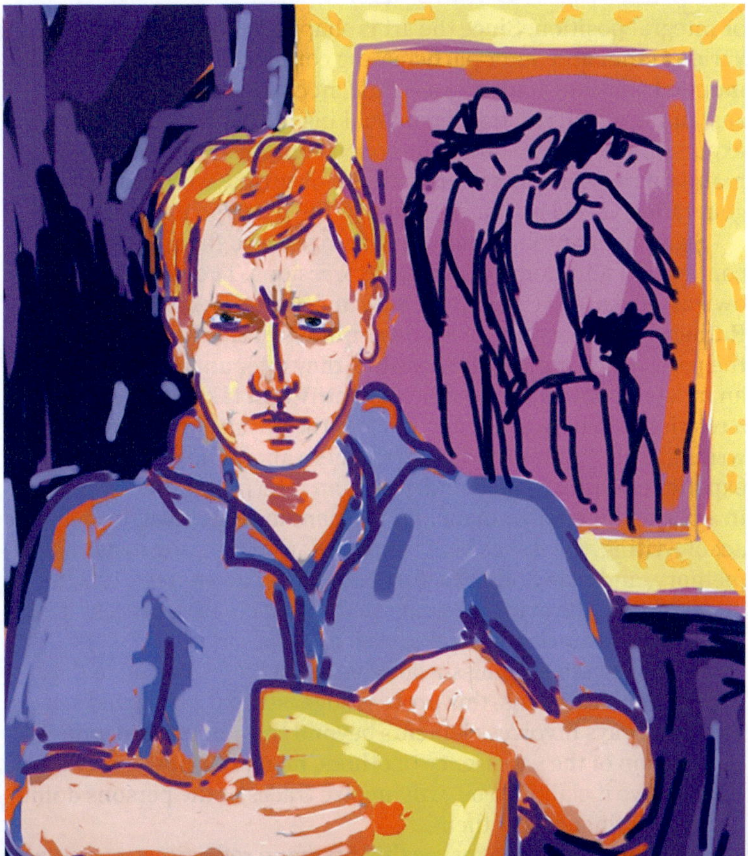

Figure 3.2: Shaun McNiff, *Finger Painting*, 2022. Digital iPad painting. © Shaun McNiff.

I have suggested, "every picture I make contains elements of self-portraiture" (1988, p. 139, 2009). In my experience, the empirical acts of intentional self-portraiture, especially when sustained in different artworks over time, suggest an intermediate or integral position. Since the art is shaped by the interplay of various inner and outer participating conditions within distinct moments in time, it manifests constant change and variation while sustaining a focus on the person making it who like the artistic expressions is never static. The concrete art evidence, however, maintains a relatively stable presence over time while reliably generating varied responses and new life when people engage it.

Significant autobiographical writings throughout history confirm the autonomy of artistic expressions. They stand on their own as works of art and create new and changing forms of life. Rather than presenting exact descriptions of a particular life and the past, which may not be possible, they offer an interpretation, an independent and self-sufficient entity that takes shape through a relationship between reflection and the physical process of writing. This applies to what I write here about the history of my experience with artistic inquiry. It is an interpretation taking place in a particular environment and moment in time, given form by the act of writing, the issues being explored, the changing dynamics of memory, and many other factors beyond my awareness. It is the material text, the evidence generated by the creative process, that persists as an autonomous expression.

In addition to helping social science get its science up to date with integral relations, this process suggests that purported self-inquiry always involves elements beyond the person, and any exploration of the experience of others, no matter how impersonal or objective it claims to be, will involve traces of the persons doing it and be influenced by them.

Over time, I came to realize that firsthand reflections on my own creative process might be more direct than secondhand discussions with others about their experience, although both clearly have value and contribute to the overall inquiry. I also appreciated the missed opportunity in not including my own art process in the doctoral research, in keeping with my later definition of art-based research—*the use of artistic expression as a primary mode of inquiry by the person doing the research, alone and/or with others.*

This instance of not doing art-based research is among the most formative experiences in the development of my understanding of the challenges to be faced in advancing this approach to inquiry. It never occurred to me at the time because my assumptions about what constitutes research were generally aligned with conventional practice, which is continued today in academic and professional institutions.

The poet Vincent Ferrini (1913–2007) often spoke to me about the significance of timing in relation to seeing clearly. All my work in the 1970s was anticipating and establishing foundations for art-based research, but I had not yet fully grasped the possibility of a distinctly artistic way of doing it. As Vincent wrote in his play *Shadows Talking*, spoken by a character, incidentally with my full name—"If you could forget/who you think you are/you might catch up with/what you really are/& can't see" (Ferrini, 1991, p. 42).

Fortunately, I did "catch up" or more accurately, art-based research caught me, and helped me see, and discover, what I had been doing organically in an ongoing process of inquiry, where the transformative processes often take shape outside conscious thought. Natural experiments, like creative discovery, tend to operate ahead of the reflecting mind. I have learned that there is an inherent purpose to the whole complex of contributing elements: a gestating community of creation that does its synthesizing and preparation of consciousness in advance of discovery. While I may not know the outcome of the work, sustained commitment to the process of creation (McNiff, 1998b), and its often wily and challenging ways, is unequivocal.

The creative process is an intelligence that tends to do its best work outside the lines of intentional thought. It moves, changes, often in unexpected, and what Alfred North Whitehead described as "accidental"[3] ways, and is never fixed. Like a stream, it is a force of nature that originates and is shaped through responses to surrounding conditions within a thoroughly reciprocal process of creation. My artistic expression tends to respond to life conditions and the work I am doing. The resulting process informs the development of art, which in turn furthers insight into experience and ongoing work with others. In the case of my personal inquiry, I may be the primary participant, but I am affected by experiences and contributing factors that often significantly influence the process outside my awareness within a more comprehensive inner and outer ecology of creation (McNiff, 2023d, 2025).

Completing a natural art experiment 50 years later

I like to think that artistic expression operates like a point-person, "a few steps ahead" of conscious awareness, and gives us the opportunity to realize an integration of the complete process. As my artist colleague Linda Klein said regarding her work, "we never know the end at the beginning" (personal communication, n.d.), and this premise is fundamental to my recommendations for the future of art-based research and discovery. Since art and life are never-ending, as a student recently said to me, we can approach the term "end" as an artistic outcome and realization. In the poem *Little Gidding*, T. S. Eliot expands the discussion, saying that ends can be present in beginnings but not always known (2024).

Generally, the creative process operates with some degree of temporal continuity and completeness in a particular time and place, in sync with the making of an artwork rather than a lifetime of exploration—which is significant in relation to artistic inquiry within academic settings, as discussed here, where there is ideally a distinct start and finish.

As I have discovered, there is no time limit to catching up with the point persons of art who offer both short and long-term insights—if we stay connected to artistic inquiry as a lifelong process. Hindsight is, as I have written, a "viewpoint on process" (McNiff, 1998b, p. 17), suggesting a positive spin on Diderot's *l'esprit d'escalier*, which tends to be associated with missed opportunities.

In retrospect, the exhibition of paintings at the final meeting with my doctoral committee, as encouraged by my advisor, anticipated what has become a primary feature of art therapy practice today that I did not fully realize at the time. The process could have been the focus of a doctoral study, but clearly, the motivation research was something I needed to do at the time in relation to my efforts to understand the sources of artmaking and offer evidence documenting flawed psychological approaches to the interpretation of artistic expressions.

The exhibit showed art that I made in response to my experience with others in a hospital art therapy studio. Working together with artists in the studio, where they were spontaneously drawing and painting portraits and pictures responding to other people and their environment, ultimately led me to join them.

In addition to the subject matter of the paintings representing people and the hospital environment, a more natural and expressive manner of expression took shape through my cooperation with the hospital artists. I was inspired by their art, and they became a primary artistic influence. They painted one another, drew and painted me, and I did the same in response to them (Figures 3.3–3.6). Graduate student interns were also creating together with the hospital artists and responding to them with paintings, photography, video, poems, music, dance,

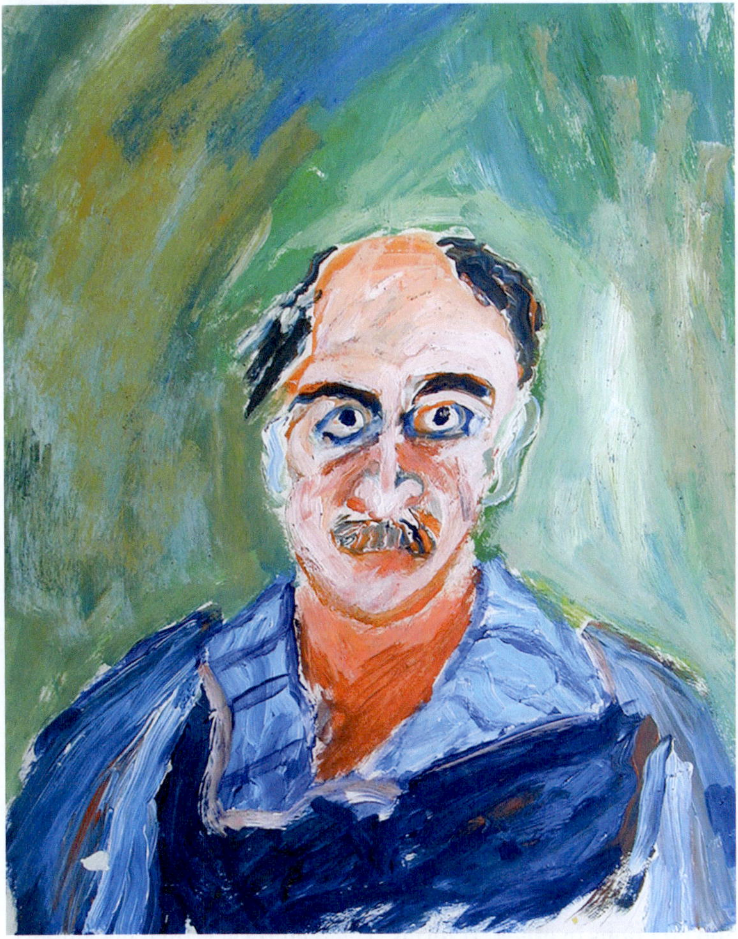

Figure 3.3: Priscilla, *Portrait of Christopher*, mid-1970s. Acrylic on paper. 18 in. × 29 in. © Shaun McNiff.

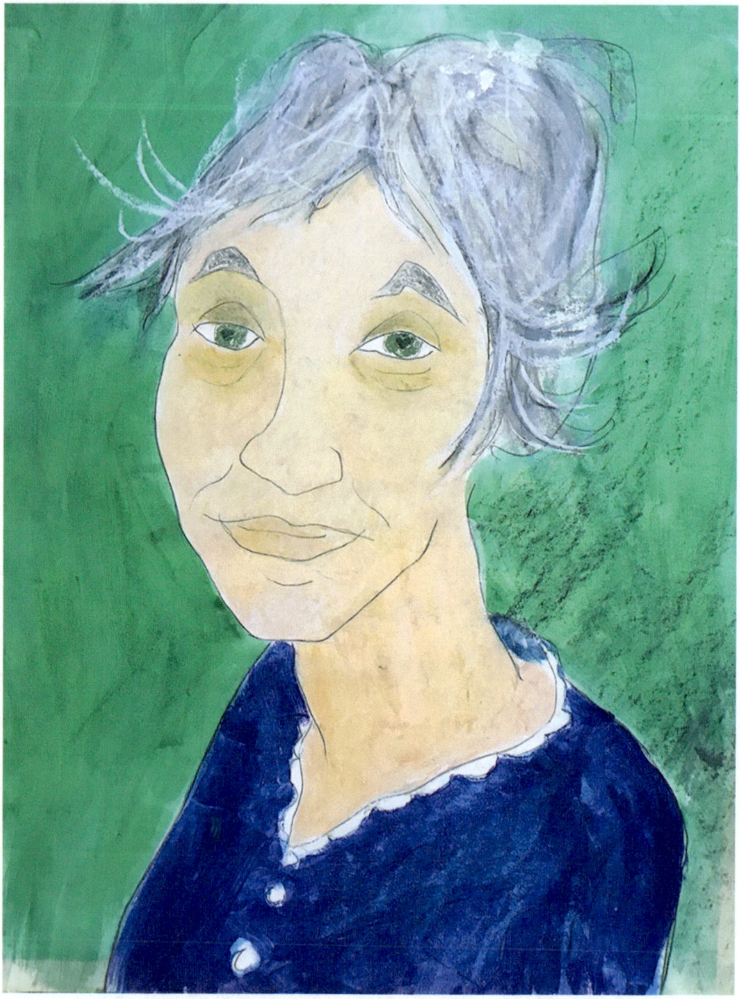

Figure 3.4: Shaun McNiff, *Mary*, mid-1970s. Pencil, oil pastel, and tempera on paper. 18 in. × 24 in. © Shaun McNiff.

and creations in other art forms. The reciprocal artmaking, often initiated by the hospital residents, affirmed the persons making the art and those portrayed, while the artistic creations offered

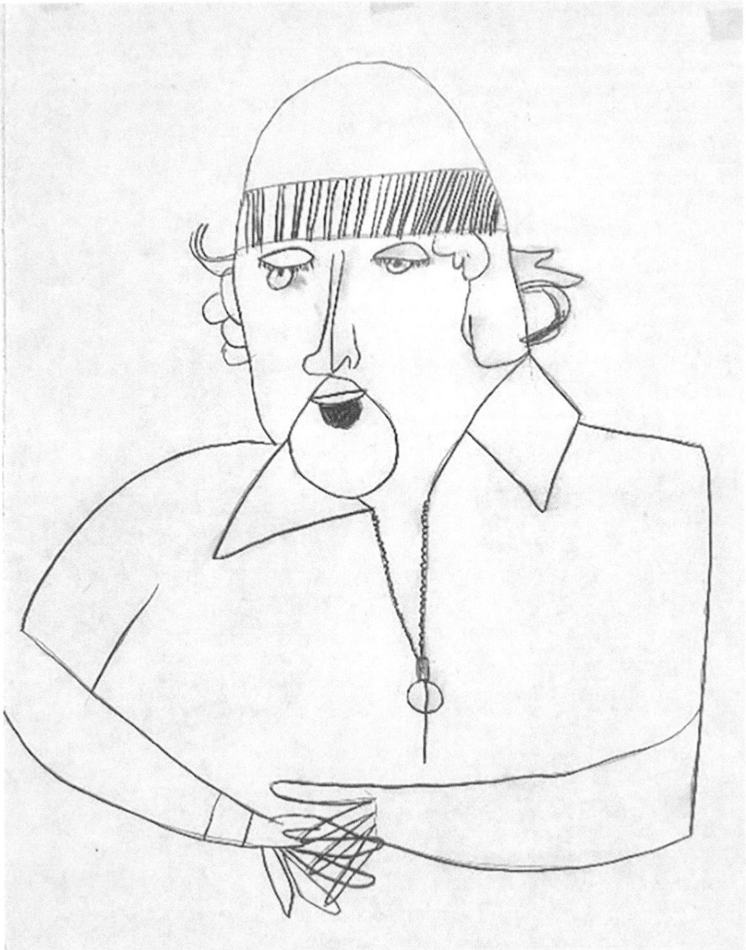

Figure 3.5: Christopher, *Portrait of Shaun McNiff*, mid-1970s. Pencil on paper. 18 in. × 29 in. © Shaun McNiff.

tangible and lasting evidence of the process. They started what I am only now appreciating as an ongoing natural art experiment.

In the mid-1970s, we were anticipating a primary method of current art therapy practice. It was all happening naturally,

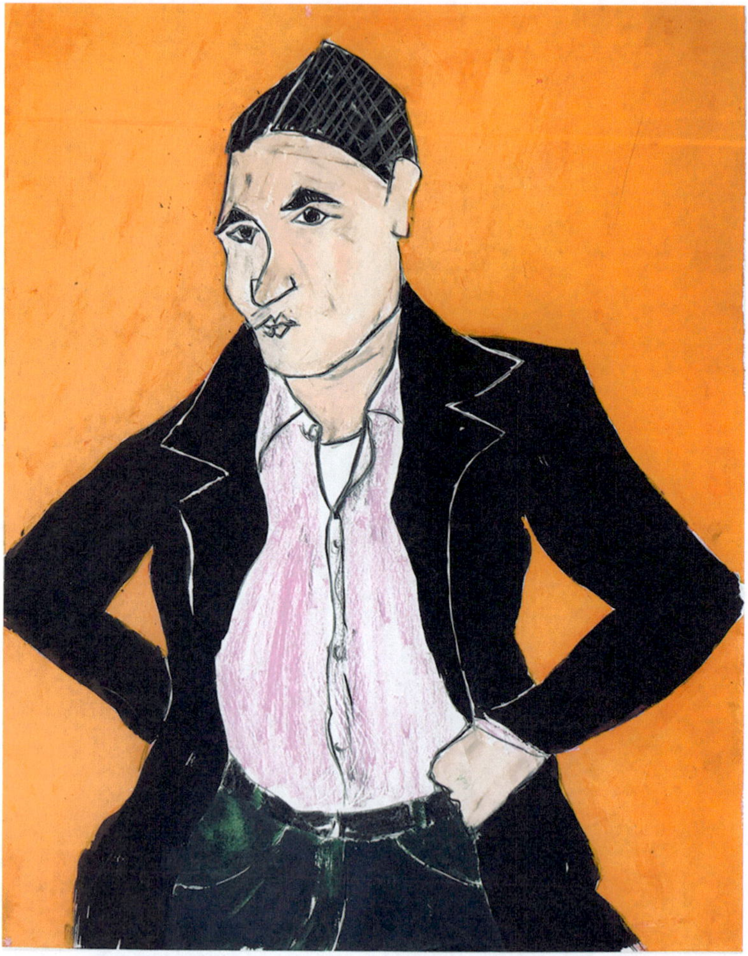

Figure 3.6: Shaun McNiff, *Danvers Man*, mid-1970s. Pencil, wax crayon, and acrylic on paper. 17 in. × 22.5 in. © Shaun McNiff.

unplanned, and in response to people working together in a hospital studio. I look upon what we did as manifesting a way of working that transcends any one of us, in keeping with the earlier discussion about the origins and practice of art-based research.

The interactive art process emerged and presented itself, and we responded as others continue to do today.

B. F. Skinner, as discussed earlier, might have been interested in understanding how the studio environment influenced and reinforced behavior, and the more general emphasis on responding artistically to immediate conditions/stimuli, all of which suggest the empirical credibility of certain aspects of stimulus-response theories. Also, in relation to my art motivation research and earlier conclusions about multiple motives and an ongoing interplay among them, I am now appreciating Kurt Lewin's emphasis on the "fields" of our present experience as sources of motivation. These contextual influences were not at the forefront of my thinking in the doctoral study, which was focused on the person making the art.

Lewin, who was Arnheim's teacher at the University of Berlin, introduced the idea of "psychological ecology" (1943, pp. 306–309). In keeping with the core premise of Gestalt psychology, where the whole is more than a collection of parts, he felt that a person's inimitable experience and character interacted with immediate environmental influences, which I describe as an "ecology of creation." Like Lewin, I approach artistic expression as a dynamic interplay of participating forces and sensibilities, both personal and environmental. We create together with inner and outer elements, all of which characterize the art I made together with, and in response to, the artists in the hospital studio, and the same applies to their creations.

Looking back, I see how the art we made showed the way to future possibilities. The mutual painting experience was one of numerous methods taking shape organically. In relation to the practice of art-based research, this example underscores the importance of *seeing* the significance and potential of what is showing itself to us, systemically reflecting on it, documenting the process, and hopefully presenting the work to others. And since creative expression is a wellspring of invention, it is fertile ground for natural art experiments. Hopefully, this book will help to further the understanding of how this might take place.

Art Alchemies

In the late 1970s, after starting a burgeoning graduate program committed to the use of all art forms in therapy and education, I continued to ask the question first posed when I became involved with art in therapy—How art heals? It was clear that art healing happened in my experience with people living in a state mental hospital environment, where making art and having it taken seriously by others affirmed the human dignity and abilities of the artists, and the public showing of their work in galleries and art museums offered convincing evidence that helped to correct the stigma associated with mental illness.

Although I may have been furthering public understanding of how art heals within a professional mental health context, I had not systematically explored the process in relation to my own art. Having just turned 30 and committed to making art, I was struggling with the constant graduate school meetings, which felt disconnected from creative expression and nature. Instinctively, I began to make drawings in the meetings that responded to the people attending and the immediate environment, realizing that nature was everywhere and art could be too (Figure 3.7).

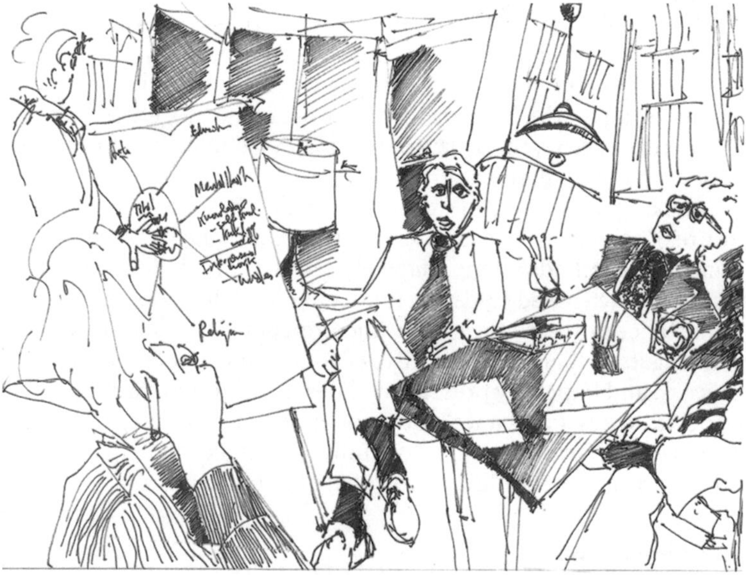

Figure 3.7: Shaun McNiff, *Deans Council, Cambridge Massachusetts*, 1979. Pen on paper. 8.5 in. × 11 in. © Shaun McNiff.

I soon realized that by responding to the existential conditions through art, I changed my perception of them. Rather than being a distraction, the process of drawing people and objects in the meeting rooms increased my concentration and sense of presence. The work can be viewed as an extension of my art motivation research and led to realizing how more challenging forms of art healing similarly involve engaging and transforming problematic conditions, crises, and afflictions into affirmations of life.

I continued with artmaking in meetings while serving on the Board of the American Art Therapy Association (Figure 3.8) and in various other professional situations.

Colleagues were supportive and intrigued (and maybe appreciated how it settled me down). Outside the meetings, I developed the drawings into large paintings, called the series *Art Alchemies*, and exhibited the work at the national art therapy conference and other art settings, including the Hartford Art School and the Addison Gallery of American Art (Figure 3.9).

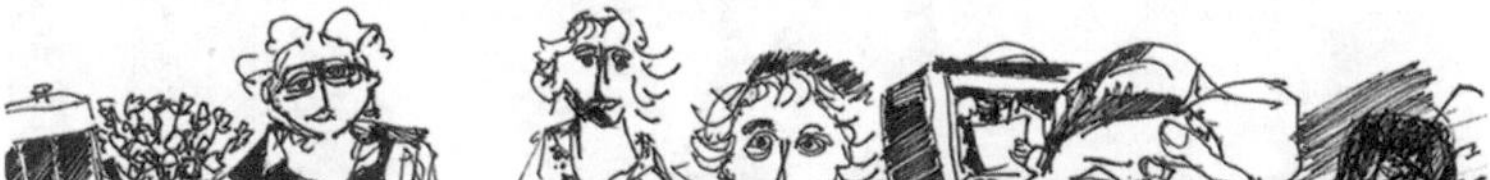

Figure 3.8: Shaun McNiff, *Robert's Rules, Board Meeting, Washington, DC*, 1979. Pen on paper. 8.5 in. × 11 in. © Shaun McNiff.

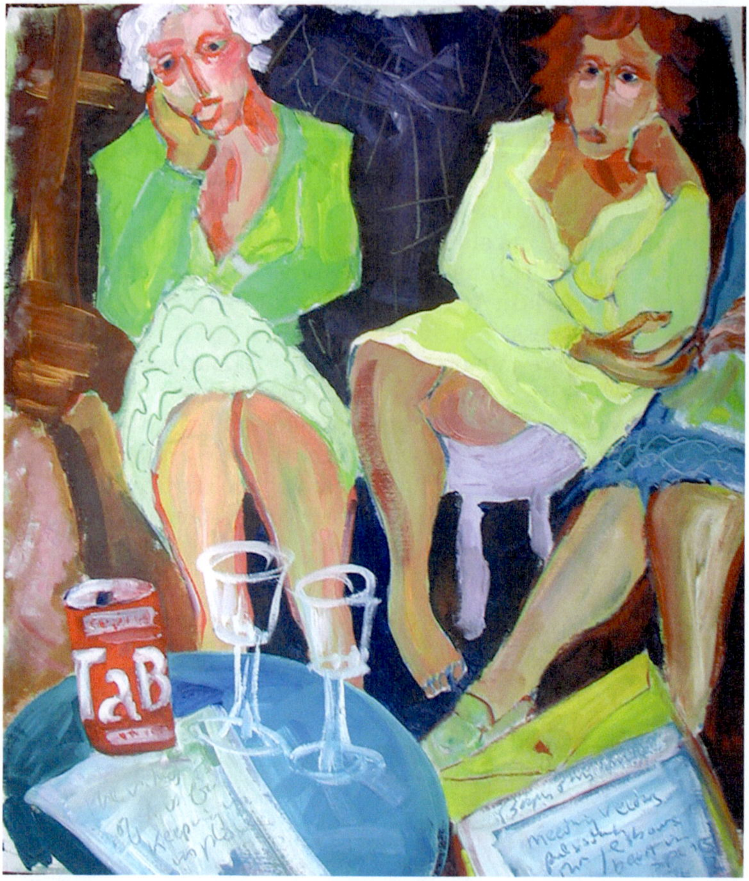

Figure 3.9: Shaun McNiff, *Late Night AATA Board Meeting*, 1979. Acrylic on canvas. 25.5 in. × 30.5 in. © Shaun McNiff.

The *meeting art* was not necessarily concerned with discomforts, but rather focused on the people, their postures and expressions, the large tables covered with papers and cups, the surrounding space and other features—all suggesting an aesthetic appreciation of the situations, a transformation of my feelings about the meetings, which took on a different significance for me, now exuding life and community.

Albeit, in many of the works, EXIT signs appear over doorways. Public and institutional rooms are required to have the signs, and I think I was more concerned with their formal features and the word itself than getting out. As I have said, where many artists sharpen their pencils to head into the external world of nature, I was looking forward to meetings as artistic inspiration.

In addition to the meetings, I began to take other areas of discomfort and respond to them with art. With particularly difficult conditions, I approached my engagements with them as an art process modeled by conceptual art colleagues, documenting the experience with photographs and other creative reflections. It worked. My intention was simply to make art in response to these situations and conflicts, exploring the idea of art healing firsthand in my own experience, with no thoughts about formal research. However, in retrospect, it was all emerging as a significant art-based natural experiment, generating considerable art evidence that appeared to impact others when it was publicly shown.

In response to my questions as to whether art heals, and how, which have been sustained over the past 55 years, the personal experimentation confirmed how artistic expression engages uneasiness and puts it to work as a motivating and transformative force, and hence the use of the term *art alchemy*. Negative conditions generated creative energy, and the meetings became a source of imagination. As I discovered, the artworks also transmitted their "art medicines," conveyed by their various expressive features as I contemplated them.

The process of making the art involved complete engagement and concentration, a contemplative process focused on the external environment, and I consistently found that I felt stimulated and better afterwards. Although the experience was multi-faceted, and there are no doubt inherent features to it that I did not perceive then, nor now, the pervasive feeling was one of change, transformation, vitalization, and social engagement. Generally, there was a sense of satisfaction even if the resulting painting might need further attention or reworking and this is perhaps a result of acting, doing something in response to a difficulty, rather than being immobilized by it.

The art object was a vital and necessary contributor to the process, an integral partner. My actions were responsive to it, and the interaction generated a new, autonomous life form, which contrasts with the one-sided emphasis that some give to process alone, shunning the products and *evidence* that emerges. To this day, decades later, the art objects act upon me, suggest new possibilities for creation, and sustain the conversation as to how art heals. These dynamics, identified through my direct experience with artistic expression, coincide with the definition of healing as a transformative process of integration that furthers well-being, making whole, easing affliction, and/or discovering how to live productively with it.

It can be asked whether art always heals? Whether it sometimes furthers disturbance and pain? Does a focus on healing transformation have a shadow dimension? Am I advocating a one-sided, feel-good position that denies destructive and chaotic aspects of creation?

Years ago, my college professor, Terence Netter (2024; McNiff, 2024), wrote to me and said that he was intrigued with my art therapy work since as he said, his art process would reliably tear him apart (McNiff, 1992, p. 62). The communication affirmed how art healing can often include pain, turmoil, and breaking as a condition of creating anew, or as Rudolf Arnheim said to me, chaos can be a "non-linear" precondition for the creation of a new order (McNiff, 2007, p. 141).[4] In *Entropy and Art* (1971), he supported what Carl Rogers described as a "formative tendency" (1978), also called a "morphic tendency" by Lancelot Whyte (1974), which continuously makes new life from tension and entropy—a concept derived from the Greek *entropia*, suggesting transformation rather than its association with disorder.

In introducing others to creative expression, I have witnessed how it often elicits great fear, vulnerability, agitation, and even the terror Rainer Maria Rilke connects with beauty in *Duino Elegies* (McNiff, 2023b). And in my experience, the depth and alchemical transformations of artistic expression frequently correlate with the energetic force of disturbance and tension. As Theodore Roethke wrote: "In a dark time, the eye begins to see" (2023) or as Elinor Gadon, the art historian who studied world religions, said to me: "The transformative experience is one of going beyond the fear of Kali to a love of Kali" (McNiff, 2023c).

In my work with others, I never intentionally introduce these tensions and disturbing forces of creation, which reliably present themselves for engagement when the context is safe and supportive of authentic expression. Based on my experience with many thousands of people throughout the world, fears, resistance, and doubt are common elements that the art process can engage and transform. In keeping with the ancient healing principle, the toxin becomes the anti-toxin and invariably catalyzes creative expression.

From this perspective, I can give thanks to my struggles since they have reliably helped to generate creative discovery, often involving a slow and steady cooking, in which the various ingredients stew, mix, dissolve, and reconfigure grievances and expectations. There is a certain breaking down and reshaping that tends to happen through dreams and artistic processes, often startling and agitating, a crucible of creation that suggests the way forward. In relation to practice, solo or with the support of others, the key is staying with the process, trusting it (McNiff, 1998b).

These transformative features of art healing tend to characterize the complete creative process and therefore it can be asked whether they also apply to art-based research. I believe they do and may be considered as defining qualities, especially in relation to the emphasis given here on the non-linear, spontaneous, and often unpredictable intelligence of artmaking, where difficulties and a certain degree of chaos may generate the formative momentum for a "new order." The forms emerging from the gestating art process ideally offer a new research outcome and as I have emphasized, its quality and impact will correspond to the effectiveness and artfulness of presentation, which will be discussed in greater detail.

As demonstrated throughout this text, we often do not yet fully see the directions taking shape unawares through an osmosis of consciousness in our lives. Open-ended artistic exploration offers a way for the research path to emerge and present itself. The process is another fundamental and distinguishing feature of artistic inquiry, affirming the importance of free and unplanned exploration in giving form to emergent elements. In contrast to controlled procedures that define scientific research, art offers the space for discovery to emerge naturally, ahead of conscious thought. The gestating process of creation gathers and shapes elements of experience into new insights and expressions. This artistic intelligence is a primary rationale for the existence of artistic and applied art disciplines and must be sustained in their research.

Personal artistic expression can advance professional understanding

> *I'm always highly irritated by people who imply that writing fiction is an escape from reality. It is a plunge into reality and it's very shocking to the system.*
>
> Mary Flannery O'Connor (1969, pp. 77–78)

A significant change in my work leading to the integration of art and research happened during the late 1980s when I was increasingly uncomfortable using the art of other people in my writing. At the time, I was working with graduate students and others in studio groups throughout the world. Remarkable things were happening and many new discoveries regarding methods of practice were taking shape, but I was reluctant to ask participants if I could show their art or describe their experiences in my writing, lectures, or teaching, and even worse suggest the use of pseudonyms, often used to ensure confidentiality, which conversely would not acknowledge their contributions.

It soon became clear that my practice was an ongoing process of research that kept renewing and advancing my work. It was never about me alone. Just being able to work together with talented students and people in training groups and open studios was a gift, and it became inconceivable to use them and their art for the benefit of something other than what we agreed to do within the sanctum of the studio.

When we earlier exhibited and publicly showed the art made by artists in the state hospital studio at the Addison Gallery of American Art (McNiff, 1972, 1974), I not only had their permission, but some wanted the outside world to see and appreciate their expression. They hoped to be perceived as artists contributing to their immediate community and society. The hospital, with its strict privacy protocols, and the families of the artists, supported showing the art—without the stereotypic pathology focus—believing this could significantly benefit their family members while helping to change perceptions of mental health and the role art can play in furthering well-being.[5] I also had close and sustained working relationships with the hospital artists, all of which made for a distinctly different context than my relationships with students and others who participated in my studios.

Regarding my work with students and participants in studio groups, I realized that fiction could enable me to describe experiences where a particular character could become a composite of what I learned from many people (McNiff, 1988). Contrary to being unreal, fiction could heighten the expression of reality.[6] I began to appreciate how literal case studies have fictive and selective dimensions, all filtered and transformed by those giving the accounts, saying as much about them as the persons they describe. Therefore, why not present the whole as fiction, especially if the impact of the text is going to be determined by the usefulness of the ideas presented and the extent to which they resonate with the experience and needs of readers. Fiction enabled me to get close to the processes and situations I was exploring, as well as the people involved, through empathy and making their experiences my own, with the individual characters and situations embodying and articulating experience with a diverse community of people.

However, as a person working extensively with actual art objects, fiction as I approached it did not allow for this. I could not take an artistic expression made by another person, in my view a living entity intimately related to the artist, and attribute it to a fictional character. I decided I could use my own art in my books to illustrate the art processes I was exploring. My purpose had increasingly moved away from literal descriptions of other people, and toward explications of principles and methods of practice, all of which I could demonstrate, perhaps more directly and completely through my own expressions and reflections on them, which do have significant imaginal qualities.

Ultimately, the value of everything that a person generates through artistic inquiry is assessed by the criteria applied to determinations of quality in all art. As previously stated, does it transcend the purely personal and connect to the experience and needs of others? And in terms of being useful to more general professional communities, will it help to advance and perfect practice? Will it inspire others to become involved with their experimentation?

While working with people in various international studio sessions during the 1980s and 1990s, I continued to make my own art in response to what we were doing. I wrote *Depth Psychology*

Art (1989) as a demonstration of this process, which once again emerged instinctively rather than as a "conscious plan" (McNiff, 1989, p. 8). I felt the need to move on from my position as a dean in higher education with its confining repetitions, and focus completely on teaching, art, and research.

It was the first time an art therapist published personal art in this way (Figures 3.10 and 3.11). I felt that self-inquiry was a prerequisite of depth, which could be embodied through artistic expressions and that paradoxically our most intimate and authentic expressions further understanding of shared human experience.

At the time, I did not know C. G. Jung's yet to be published *The Red Book: Liber Novus* (2009), created between 1913 and 1930, a privately held masterpiece I have described as "the most elegant object ... in art therapy's history" (McNiff, 2011, p. 145). Jung would not describe what he did as art and described it as a creative exploration. Nevertheless, in my view, it is a preeminent example of art-based research, conducted long before the term originated, where Jung used personal inquiry and experimentation to shape and perfect his methods of practice with others.

In publishing *Depth Psychology of Art*, I was well aware of potentially offering the work, with often unusual imagery expressing inner tensions, to those seeking the psychopathology of expression. No doubt these factors influenced the heirs of Jung, who kept *Liber Novus* unpublished in a bank vault after his death, and he would only show it confidentially to help others understand the process.

To my knowledge, the art diagnosticians kept their distance from my book, and other art therapists began to openly show their art and integrate it into their publications (Allen, 1995; Moon, 1990, 1992). Although the inclusion of my paintings was intended as a demonstration of the depth psychology of art illustrated by artistic expressions made in response to practice, the major practical, and unintended, outcome may have been establishing a precedent for the use of personal artistic expression in all aspects of practice and research. In recent years, the art therapy field has embraced the use of artistic expression by therapists in professional supervision as a mode of reflection, establishing an integral consistency with the nature and depth of the discipline (Byrne & Fenner, 2023; Fish, 2016; Nash, 2019).

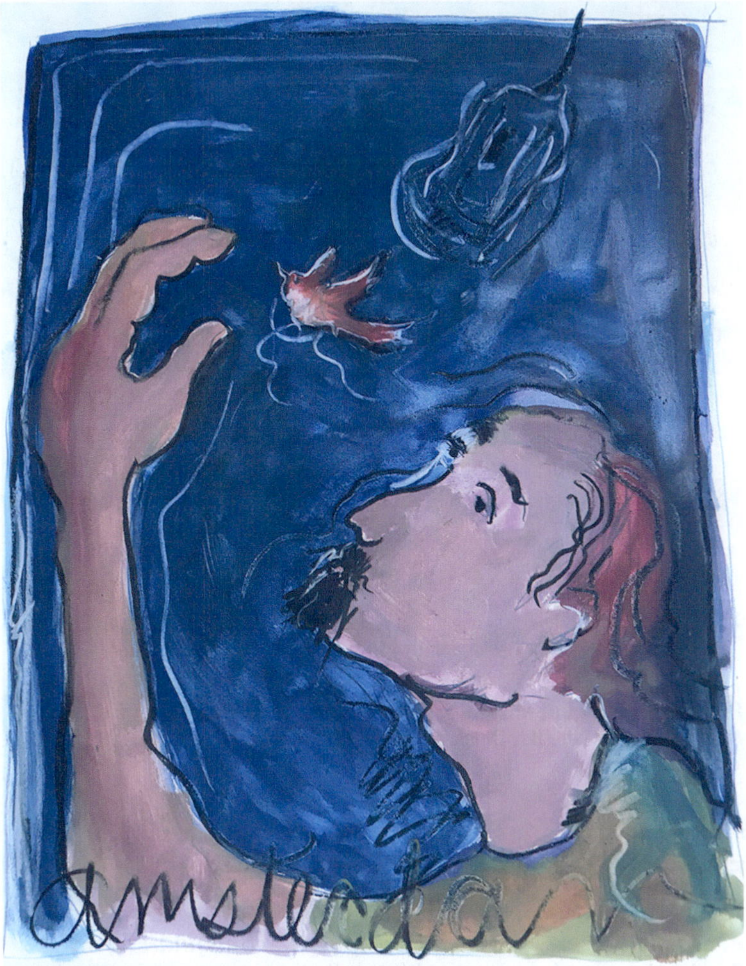

Figure 3.10: Shaun McNiff, *Out of the Cage, Amsterdam, The Netherlands*, 1988. Pencil, oil pastel, and tempera on paper. 19.5 in. × 25.5 in. © Shaun McNiff. The Amsterdam training group was taking place in the studio of Annette Brederode, which contained a collection of antique bird cages. I identified with the bird being set free.

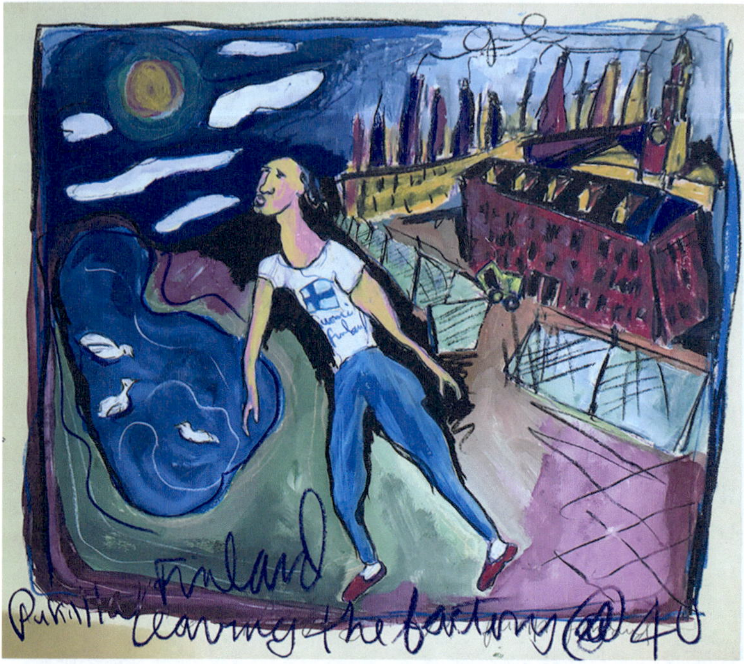

Figure 3.11: Shaun McNiff, *Leaving the Factory, Pukilla Series, Finland*, 1988. Pencil, oil pastel, and tempera on paper. 22 in. × 25.5 in. © Shaun McNiff.

Firsthand experimentation with methods of practice

Art as Medicine: Creating a Therapy of the Imagination, my first book to reach a broad public audience, presents systematic experimentation with a method of artistic practice. As with *Depth Psychology of Art*, the book included an extended artistic inquiry (1992, pp. 143–226), in this case involving imaginal dialogue with my paintings and drawings. The process of responding to an image with imaginal, or poetic, dialogue was in sync with integrating art forms as advanced by the graduate program I established. We were responding to visual art, for example, with movement, performance, vocal improvisation, poetic writing, and various other art forms. The process of responding to art with art was ongoing. We repeatedly discovered that these art responses were more intimate and reliably insightful than the usual narrative explanations and descriptions. Imaginal dialogue approached artworks in all media and not just visual art, as living and autonomous figures, partners in creation. As mentioned previously, I liken artistic expressions to offspring—closely related to, but distinctly other than the persons who made them.

In *Art as Medicine*, I describe how we shift from talking *about* creations to talking *with* them (1992). The conversational mode relaxes the ego position and its controls, stimulating many new responsive and imaginative dimensions of speech and discovery.

I became involved with image dialogue through my work with James Hillman beginning in the early 1980s and building on Jung's use of active imagination and the process of "personifying" images. In one of our meetings, when responding to a painting of a male figure, Jim said: "Let's stop laying trips on him and see what he has to say for himself." The quality of the conversation changed dramatically. It was more alive, direct, emotional, imaginative, poetic, dramatic, and devoid of abstract concepts. In reflecting on our inquiry, he said:

> The painting is teaching me how to look at it. It's saying, "Drop what you are coming in with, your biases. This is the way I am, and I present myself this way" .... The picture reveals its own set of criteria as we look at it.
>
> (personal communication, ca. 1990)

This observation is consistent with Rudolf Arnheim's emphasis on how an artwork's structural qualities generate its own expression, which is to be distinguished from anthropocentric projections attributed to it—what he described as "words derived from human states of mind to describe objects, processes" (1974, p. 452). As Jim and I experimented with image dialogue, it was clear that our speech was a new imaginative creation made by responding to the autonomous expression of the painting, a dialogical exchange.

Art as Medicine experimented with ways of being more attentive, imaginative, and sensitive in engaging art objects. In addition to me being reluctant to engage other people as "human subjects" or use their art for my inquiry, personal artistic explorations expanded creative possibilities (Figure 3.12). I could

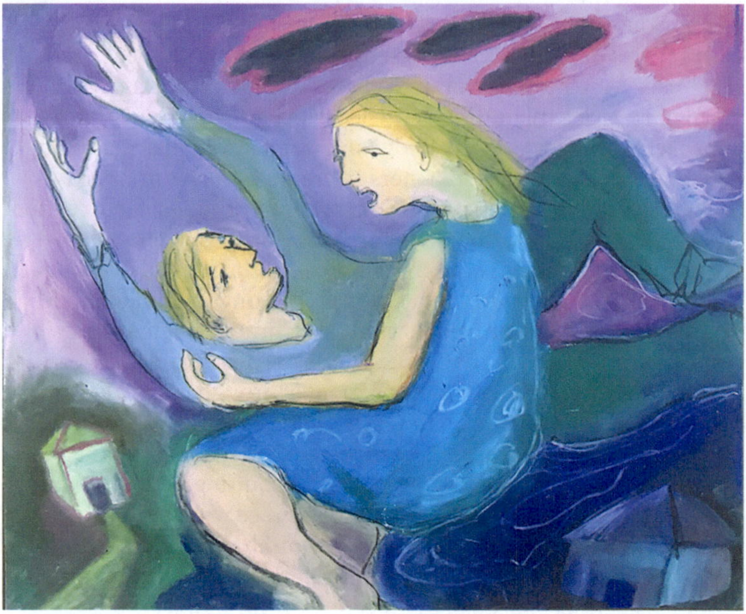

Figure 3.12: Shaun McNiff, *Letting Go—Stations of Psyche, Wienacht, Switzerland*, 1991. Oil pastel and pencil on paper. 14 in. × 17 in. © Shaun McNiff.

experiment in ways not ethically possible when engaging other people and their art: "I can take risks, speak freely, and publish the contents of intimate dialogue. I do not want to use another person's private expression to elucidate my methods" (McNiff, 1992, p. 4).

In addition to exploring and perfecting how a particular method works before involving others, personal experimentation offers firsthand understanding. The systematic examination of a method of artistic practice documented in *Art as Medicine* informed my work in advising doctoral research. It offered an example of how a distinctly unique artistic inquiry can both embrace the personal and transcend it in striving to be of use to others.

Of course, artistic methods tend to emerge spontaneously when engaging others, and their applications relate to endlessly different conditions, but the ability to flexibly respond to these situations is furthered by an organic and firsthand understanding of the process. In training, we call this experiential learning, and the same principles apply to research.

Plans and the *nature* of artistic intelligence

As I will describe later in this book, when discussing doctoral research, experimentation with a particular method of artistic expression is thoroughly empirical and often orientated to improving professional practice. The concrete and structured nature of the inquiry guards against intangibility, supports the creation of a doctoral proposal with clear procedures, and most importantly, successful completion of the research, all of which I continue to encourage. However, I have come to realize how carefully planned doctoral proposals, even when supporting significant changes and revisions in response to factors emerging from implementation, can limit natural experimentation and its close correspondence to the creative process.

As described earlier in reflecting on my personal artistic expression and experience in supporting others, artistic intelligence generally does not follow plans, especially linear procedures established in advance. It is a "gestating" force and ecosystem of creation that integrates a "complex" of contributing elements within artists and their environments in particular moments of time. The endlessly varied outcomes take shape in the process of artistic action, building upon successive acts sometimes by chance and accident, and often emerging in advance of the reflecting mind.

Since this description might at first seem to contradict the planning process in academic research, we can ask: Is it possible to encourage both planned and open-ended artistic inquiry within formal academic research? Are there ways to integrate the approaches?

In giving a conference keynote address on art-based research at a State University of New York campus, and after emphasizing the significance of concise, concrete, and clear doctoral plans, I was asked by two MFA students whether doctoral research can be done through open-ended and intuitive painting, consistent with their studio work. In many ways, they were posing the antithesis to everything I had recommended in the lecture, and I have come to embrace the question as essential to the future of art-based research.

I was sympathetic to the students based on my personal history as described here, but as a person working with many doctoral advisees, and with a responsibility to help them complete the work with excellence in a timely way, we begin by establishing a plan. I have always encouraged open-ended art making as a way of generating and discovering a direction, focus, question, or issue to be explored and almost universally the doctoral plan that we carefully shape together, is tied to this formative process. On several occasions, while pursuing research according to an approved plan, unexpected events, needs, and difficulties emerged—an occurrence that frequently characterizes the art process—and the direction was changed, sometimes significantly, and opening new possibilities and discoveries, as with the history of unsuccessful experiments in science. Thus, the plan is a flexible structure offering a starting point which can be altered and transformed consistent with the making of art—as I have emphasized, the "best things happen" often contrary to our expectations and plans (2015).

If I put aside my history of dissertation advising involving various formal and programmatic requirements beyond my control, together with my vigilance in helping students complete their work within the academic system, and approach art-based research without institutional structures, the question posed by the SUNY students is pivotal. I keep returning to it. They were essentially asking whether art-based research can be grounded in the nonlinear, dynamic, and unpredictable artistic intelligence informed by *responses* to the changing and distinctive moments of a person's life. It does not simply follow procedure, even those we may formulate ourselves versus institutional prescriptions established in advance.

With informal research outside the academy, there is no question, as confirmed by my own practice shown here, that open-ended and unplanned art-based research can be done. And more complete integration with artistic processes will further future relevance. Research within the academy presents challenges that will be addressed.

In reflecting again on my history in shaping methods of working with people in my studio groups, I see how one of my most formative experiences involved an experimental group that operated in a way that can be likened to the approach proposed by the SUNY students.

In my work developing the first graduate program to integrate all forms of artistic expression in therapy and education, faculty were learning together with students within our more general experimental environment that often characterized the era. I was intrigued by group improvisations where free and natural expressions with movement, enactment, voice, chant, and percussion, consistently manifested a tendency to naturally converge into rhythmic structures and common streams of expression. The patterns occurred in both small groups and large gatherings of over 100 people. Leaders offered minimal direction and encouraged each person to make natural movements and sounds, which merged into the collective that carried us all. There was powerful creative energy, a force inviting participation and contribution to something larger than oneself, a supportive and thoroughly natural community of creation. I wanted to understand it and become more comfortable in making a place for it in my work with groups, where I similarly encouraged creative expression to emerge spontaneously.

I felt an atavistic depth in these spontaneous, unscripted, and authentic experiences in Cambridge, Massachusetts, that were initiated exclusively in the present moment uncontrolled by extraneous aspects, recorded music, etc. While the group improvisations made no reference to, nor attempted to replicate nor adopt, practices or traditions beyond themselves, I questioned if there was continuity with the larger human community, now and in the past. Do they correspond to an inherent structure of nature? Do they in any way manifest physical laws, the "rhythms and patterns" of life, such as the law of gravitation, as described by Richard Feynman (1967, p. 13).

My orientation then, and now, is a sense of the interconnectedness of life and human experience. In college, I studied world religions, with a focus on East Asian traditions with Thomas Berry (1999, 2015). I read Mircea Eliade (1961, 1964) and others who helped me explore how what I do and experience in a particular time and place might relate to the larger world community as contrasted to the exclusive reduction of experience to various cultural, historical, and conceptual categories and circumscribed entities. As Mary Caroline Richards declared: "Ideas do not belong to people. Ideas live in the world as we do" (1989, p. 28), and Rudolf Arnheim had always considered how specific art expressions manifest universal forces.

While embracing the individual integrity of artistic expressions, are there shared qualities? Significant differences? Is art healing potentially accessible to people everywhere? And if so, how does it happen? Does present experience manifest human continuity, a deeply embedded basis of art healing? Can the contemplation of our present artistic expressions distill "essential features from nature" shared by others (McNiff, 1998b, pp. 100–108)?

Where I had considerable experience with the visual arts, video, creative writing, and other forms of individual art expression in groups from the start of my work in art and therapy, I was not as involved in leading groups dealing with collective movement, vocal improvisation, chant, percussion, enactment, and other spontaneous forms of communal expression, where I experienced considerable depth as a participant (Figure 3.13).

In the early years of the graduate program, a group of former students wanting to stay engaged as a community took the lead in forming what we called the Healing Lab, a weekly 2-to-3-hour

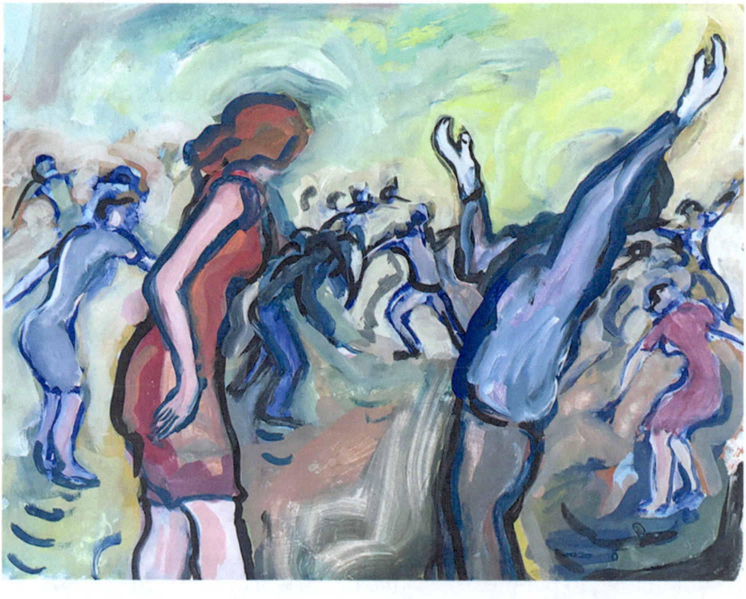

Figure 3.13: Shaun McNiff, *Dance*, ca. 2004. Tempera on paper. 19 in. × 24 in. © Shaun McNiff.

session involving spontaneous and free expression that also involved faculty. Paolo Knill, who became my closest colleague in developing what I called *total art expression*, which grew into today's professional discipline of *expressive arts therapy*, was also committed to the group, which became a vital form of practitioner research for us. He came to the graduate program from Switzerland with a background in music and, in addition to our experimental group he joined classes in other art disciplines to further his understanding of integrative art processes in therapy.

There was no designated group leader, and we worked as peers. The improvisational sessions involved open-ended and simultaneous individual improvisation in a group setting. I could experiment with new expressions, often reciprocally with other group members, in my case always in areas such as singing and vocal improvisation, where I had less experience, self-confidence, and inhibition. As I have subsequently discovered in my work over the years with others, these more vulnerable and often repressed areas tend to hold tremendous energy and potential for creative release and transformation. I had a personal history with dance and movement, and strong inclinations for percussion, enactment, and ritual, all of which were focal points of my experimentation and ultimately became fundamental to the groups I lead integrating all forms of artistic expression.

A major takeaway from this group experimentation with sound, movement, enactment, percussion, ritual, and chant was the reliable generation of a collective creative energy and relaxation that motivated and supported expression. Random and sometimes chaotic beginnings tended to consistently cohere into clear and sustained rhythms that held variations of expression. And in terms of my questions regarding transcultural practices, the experimentation corresponded to how longstanding healing processes native to disparate settings closely attuned to the natural environment, consistently involved enactment, rhythm, voice, percussion, and what we would today describe as artistic expression in a community context. The collective effort activates creative energy, an "imaginative contagion that keeps the process moving" (McNiff, 1989, p. 8).

It is important to emphasize that I have never been interested in adopting, imitating, or applying practices from another culture. My studies of world healing traditions have been concerned with shared qualities and continuities across cultures, and how my most personal experience in a particular time and place might connect to broader human phenomena. For example, when studying Celtic folk healing traditions as a visiting professor at The University of Galway in Ireland, and living in Connemara in 1979–1980, I never considered incorporating practices occurring in that region into what I do with people. My focus has always been an examination of how what I do in my distinctive ways, together with the approaches of colleagues and students, might relate to historic world practices. Whatever cultural ties I might personally have to previous generations of Celtic history, perhaps lessening today's potential accusations of cultural appropriation with regard to my research, the practices I studied were shaped in a time and place distant from the singular context and environmental conditions in which my work has emerged. Rather than imitating, I have found it valuable to study and imagine how the things we do in response to our varied life situations share qualities with the larger human community—a research direction that I feel has significant merit for the future.

In relation to my experience working internationally with art healing, I am consistently asked about cultural differences but rarely about similarities and shared humanity (McNiff, 2019b), which I continuously observe and experience. In having the opportunity to work closely with people from throughout the world over five decades, I can report the infinite variations of their individual creations, together with the common features of the creative process.

In a delayed response to the SUNY students, I say: Yes, art-based research can, and arguably should involve, free and spontaneous studio inquiry. My personal experience documents how this happens naturally when the artistic process responds to life conditions and challenging issues, demonstrated here by developing new uses of art in therapy and healing, or as I have suggested, opening to deep streams of worldwide and continuous forces of expression and art healing (McNiff, 1979, 1981, 1992, 2004).

This description of my experience with artistic inquiry suggests that personal artistic practice, in keeping with the idea of natural experiments, may be the most fundamental feature of art-based research that must be maintained into the future. The extended process happened organically when artistic inquiry was not formally recognized as research by the prevailing academic and professional standards of society. Perhaps these personal reflections can encourage creative experimentation and sustained openness to modes of inquiry outside the lines invariably drawn by hegemonic definitions as to what is, and is not, research (McNiff, 1986a, 2002, 2023d).

An outcome of the growth and wider adoption of artistic inquiry in recent years is that art-based research is often designated with different names, as described earlier. This is perhaps inevitable, and once again a manifestation of individual creations and variations as affirmed here. Differences are crucial and inherent to various forms of artistic inquiry, but hopefully emerging communities of practice and the work they do will sustain the shared purpose urged by Ross W. Prior in his previously mentioned statement. My recommendation is to support the unlimited uniqueness of artistic expression and possibilities while keeping the common, unifying, and mutually supportive, and all-inclusive commitment to natural artistic inquiry. As I continuously discover, the slipstreams of shared creative expression will carry us together and with our endlessly varied art processes.

A threat to art-based research, as it succeeds in establishing an international identity, is reliance on fixed systems and linear, step-by-step methods of practice that are already appearing, which I see as contradicting the nature of artistic expression with their continuous replication of themselves. As we know from helping others become involved with artistic expression, fear that nothing will emerge, and the angst suggested by a possible absence of clear purpose, generate a reliance on pre-existing frameworks. The following pages will consider how to affirm structure while preserving uniqueness and unpredictable discovery, in keeping with art and nature.

But first, it is necessary to address today's insistence on "evidence-based research" and how the demand can be re-visioned to include art.

Notes

1. Contemporary AI and digital coding mechanisms, programmed according to these reductionistic concepts, can potentially magnify the problematic practice. I can envision art diagnosticians presenting the standardizations as an "evidence-based" scientific procedure. As I will discuss later, the use of artificial intelligence, especially when intended to support *artistic intelligence* which can keep it grounded in the human realm of creation, will

no doubt be widely explored by artists. But this area and all of the issues it raises in terms of what it can and cannot do, including the technology's dependence on whatever pre-existing materials are programmed into it, are beyond our scope here. I can say, based on my experience prompting artificial intelligence in complex areas where I have firsthand knowledge, the results have often been superficial and inaccurate. However, I marvel at its ability to instantly access otherwise difficult to obtain content. See p. 28.

2. The *art of conversation* did serve this function. For example, in the early stages of the research I was exploring tension reduction and the movement from disorder to order as motivating forces in artistic processes. The conceptual artist Don Burgy, who was focusing on art ideas, described how his work, although striving to reduce ambiguity, was often permeated by disorder, intentional disequilibrium, and confrontation of his greatest fears. The exchange had a major impact on my thinking, ruling out the possibility of a singular source of motivation or a consistent set of factors, and influencing the final determination of multiple art motives and their different individual configurations, as with art itself (McNiff, 1977). See p. 30.
3. "In all philosophic theory there is an ultimate which is actual in virtue of its accidents. It is only then capable of characterization through its accidental embodiments" (Whitehead, 1979, p. 7). See. p. 35.
4. Michel Talagrand (in Wilkins, 2024), recipient of the 2024 Abel Prize for mathematics, affirms the formative forces within apparently random processes. See p. 46.
5. The Lieutenant Governor of the Commonwealth of Massachusetts, Donald Dwight, hosted the exhibit at the State House and visited the hospital studio; his wife, Susan Dwight, became a dedicated participant in the art therapy program together with the Governor's niece, Ford Sargent. Not long before, Frederick Wiseman's 1967 documentary *Titicutt Follies*, filmed within another Massachusetts state hospital, was banned, purportedly due to privacy concerns. In 1991, the courts approved the release of the now-celebrated film, which can be perceived as art-based research. See p. 48.
6. The psychological value and reality of fiction are emphasized by James Hillman (1983) and Patricia Leavy (2009, 2018, 2025). Leavy, whose writings explore all forms of artistic expression in research, has made significant personal contributions through her focus on fiction. See p. 49.

4

Art Is the Evidence: Persons, Process, and Creations

This is an era of "evidence-based research." In supporting the need for real and convincing evidence, I believe there is generally an absence of critical discourse about what it can be. Within the realm of research relating to human experience, institutional demands for evidence largely reduce and restrict it to "data" generated by accepted social science procedures and their accompanying theories. It is reasonable to suggest that this results in a circular pattern whereby the institutional systems controlling the definition of evidence, and its production, are reinforced.

For example, in 2007, the United Kingdom's Department of Health together with the Arts Council England published a *Prospectus for Arts and Health* describing the "evidence base" of international research documenting how "the arts have a major contribution to make to wellbeing" (Arts Council England, 2026). While concurring with the government report's affirmation of art's contributions to public health, I cannot do the same for the assumption that the healing effects of art are to be exclusively examined through allegedly scientific procedures and evidence.

In his 2010 editorial introducing the inaugural issue of the *Journal of Applied Arts & Health (JAAH)*, Ross W. Prior referred to the Prospectus and wrote: "[T]he very idea of what actually constitutes 'evidence' is a particularly interesting one, and we hope that we will see lively scholarly debate within future editions." The editorial initiated a necessary discussion and invitation to explore "what is meant by 'evidence'" (2010, pp. 4–5).

More recently, in a 2019 *JAAH* editorial written by Ross W. Prior and Mitchell Kossak, they respond to a World Health Organization, Europe report entitled *What Is the Evidence on the Role of the Arts in Improving Health and Well-Being? A Scoping Review* (World Health Organization, 2024), published right after the Journal's ten-year anniversary conference in Telford, England. As with the above-mentioned 2007 report, WHO affirmed the contributions of the arts to mental and physical health. But again, the "evidence" cited was drawn exclusively from what Prior and Kossak describe as "social science and quasi-scientific methodologies" utilizing scoping and coding technologies that "move us further away from understanding common-sense effects of the benefits of art" and "that *art itself can and has always provided the evidence*" (2019, p. 273, original emphasis).

The WHO report compellingly affirms Ross W. Prior's original call to question and debate the nature of evidence in research dealing with the effects of art on human well-being.

An evidentiary epiphany

In 2014, when writing an article for a special issue of the *Journal of Applied Arts & Health*, which grew from a 2013 conference sponsored by La Trobe University in Melbourne, Australia, I was summoned for jury duty in a district court trial. The La Trobe event was called Evidence in a different form (Rumbold et al., 2014). And my article, responding to the conference title, was entitled Art speaking for itself: Evidence that inspires and convinces (2014a).

The presiding judge at the trial addressed the potential jurors and described how the advocacy process involves the respective attorneys in making arguments to "try and persuade jurors to see evidence in a certain way." While artistic creations do contain expression within their physical structure, and do speak for themselves, the judge's instruction to the jury reinforces how direct physical evidence can be perceived differently, and that advocates will do their best to persuade and convince them to see it in particular ways as I am undertaking here.

Fortuitously, the statement helped me extricate the concept of evidence from the current research context and look at it afresh, reframed within the time-tested legal tradition and its history of "evidentiary standards," the "burden of proof," and especially the notion of concrete, non-theoretical, indisputable evidence grounded in consensually perceived fact. It is the tangible art, both the creative actions of the people involved and the outcomes they generate, that constitute the evidence of art-based research and demonstrate how art heals.

And also, the sustained credibility of the judicial process underscores the importance of considering how we perceive and interpret art evidence. Do we make perfunctory translations into pre-existing social science systems, or do we approach it artistically—doing our best to both recognize and respect its empirical presence and open ourselves to the inevitable spectrum of artistic interpretations and imaginative responses?

Art speaks for itself as "a primary source" and does not need to be treated as "data" and be translated into what can be considered, at best, "secondary" and questionably scientific formats, which cancel its presence and expression. This practice marginalizes the essential artistic process of inquiry and its empirical results. As Don Quixote said in the novel by the same name written by Cervantes, apparently and ironically the world's most translated work, reliance on translations can be likened to looking at the backside of a Flemish tapestry.

Without in any way challenging the primacy of evidence and its importance, it is appropriate to ask, what kind of evidence? This is especially significant today, when contemporary social and behavioral science avert critical assessment as to the nature of evidence and privileged methods of inquiry often reduce outcomes based on opinion and speculation to numerical measurement. As Rudolf Arnheim said to me: "Counting and measuring are fine for things that can be counted and measured" (personal communication, n.d.).

The nature and intricacies of artistic expression and its impact on human experience and relations are arguably not something to be understood by attempts to reduce the irreducible to statistical formulations. Measurement processes are fundamental throughout society, professions, and personal life, where quantification informs decisions, planning, and much of daily life. They contribute to art, especially in the social and organizational realms, in relation to examining issues and processes that lend themselves to statistical assessment. Collaboration with science can, for example, further understanding of the physiological effects of artistic expression in relation to those who create and perceive it. Art has neurological and somatic dimensions but the assumption that the evidence concerning the effects of artistic expression is to be exclusively determined by measurement of these internal and involuntary biological systems overlooks the direct, physical, and primary evidence offered by the art itself and the sensory perception of reality (Arnheim & Grundmann, 2025). Regarding cooperation with science, I have emphasized how artistic expressions may have more to do with physics and the examination of forces, energy, action and reaction (Newton's Third Law of Motion), inertia, optics, acoustics, quanta, entropy and order as studied by Arnheim (1971), and so forth.

In defining art evidence, it is important to underscore the integral relationship of persons, creative processes, and outcomes. There is a tendency, especially with the visual arts and other art forms that generate standalone works, to bifurcate "process and product." Warren Lett, with his formative experience in the temporal medium of dance and interpersonal experience, emphasized evidence presented by "the content in the process" (Lett, 2016, p. 6; McNiff, 2021b, p. 48), a position he extended to other art forms and collaboration with research "companions" (Lett et al., 2014).

Art evidence includes the people who make it. While artistic expressions have their empirical autonomy, they are extensions of their creators. When speaking of art as evidence, we refer to unique outcomes shaped by the interplay of persons, processes, and empirical creations emerging in particular moments. They include but are not limited to creative action, inner contemplation and feelings, the participation of all the senses, spontaneity and disciplined practice, instinct and critical judgment, memory, environmental influences, visions and challenges, and the formative properties and forces generated by interaction with materials of artistic expression. This complex of creation cannot be evidenced through paradigms and procedures that do not reflect its essential features.

In my supervision of art-based doctoral research, the accessibility of quality digital video and other new media has been transformative in advancing the integral relationship between art processes and outcomes while also creating permanent documentation of temporal activities, as will be discussed. But most importantly, video technology includes the presence of the persons involved and the creative action.

While the current use of new media has been a significant advance, which is prominently featured here, I do not want to limit art-based research to it and inadvertently promulgate the reliance on fixed methods that I discourage. The future of artistic inquiry will hopefully correspond to the new and ongoing manifestations of art and the evidence they present.

Clear and convincing: Artistic quality matters

"Art is the evidence" emerged as a defining feature of art-based research when I was preparing for a keynote talk to the tenth anniversary conference of the *Journal of Applied Arts & Health* in Telford, UK (McNiff, 2019a). In building on earlier writing about how quality artistic presentations will impact people and offer convincing evidence of how art heals (McNiff, 2014a, 2014b), the statement took shape. It resonated with conference delegates committed to art-based research and understanding how the process of inquiry and presentation of the research are integral to one another (Prior, 2018a, pp. 56–57). And serendipitously, the talk taking place at the anniversary event addressed the original question about the nature of evidence posed by Ross W. Prior in founding the journal.

In offering an example of art evidence from the public domain, I showed a clip from the YouTube video of the "dancing inmates" interpreting Michael Jackson's *Thriller* at the Cebu Provincial Detention and Rehabilitation Center (CPDRC), a maximum-security prison in the Philippines. One of YouTube's first viral videos, it was originally uploaded in 2007 by the prison head, Byron Garcia (2025). It offers a vivid illustration of artistic mastery and discipline, community cooperation, passionate expression, and the presence of life-affirming humanity and creation in a harsh environment.

Garcia instituted the art program to encourage physical exercise and rehabilitation in the jail. He also sought to confront the dark social and cultural legacy of imprisonment, which evokes many questions and reactions.[1]

I asked the conference delegates: If we insist upon quantification in research, how do you perceive the social impact of the millions (60 million at the time of the Telford event) of video views? Why do you think the video has generated such interest? Does the art speak for itself? How does this succinct art evidence compare to institutionally recognized forms of "evidence-based research" in furthering human understanding and appreciation of art's healing and rehabilitative potential?

In leading the closing session of the conference, Mitchell Kossak, a principal developer of art-based research and expressive arts therapy (2008, 2012, 2018, 2021), to my surprise, initiated a rhythmic repetition of my "Art is the evidence" statement, and is to be credited, together with the conference community and our host, Ross W. Prior, with giving it autonomous life. The enactment can be viewed as another spontaneous art experiment involving a community of people exploring the nature of art-based research. The communal and energizing art process, like the Healing Lab experimentation years earlier, had a tremendous impact on me. An idea, like a rhythmic process, needs community repetition to sustain itself. It became *evident* that artistic expression, a timeless mode of compelling communication, is an appropriate vehicle for presenting research involving the making of art.

In the Telford presentation, I showed how the graduate institute I established in 1974 grew from the earlier-mentioned Addison Gallery of American Art exhibition, featuring the hospital art therapy program and artists (McNiff, 1972, 1974).[2] Supported by the Massachusetts Council on the Arts and Humanities, the work of the hospital artists was shown by museums and university galleries throughout the Northeast of the United States. In addition to visual art, the Addison Gallery staff at Phillips Academy, Andover, Massachusetts, led by director Christopher Cook, a conceptual art pioneer committed to furthering the contributions of art to community and institutional life, worked with us in using video to document group and individual expressions with movement, enactment, voice, music, and creative writing, all of which I will discuss later in more detail.

First shown in 1972, the exhibition took what I had done in the hospital setting in presenting art made in studio groups to psychiatric staff, families of patients, educational training programs, and community groups to a new level. It offered the public convincing and inspirational evidence of creative abilities, enhanced by presentation in the museum environment (Figure 4.1). The exhibition and the

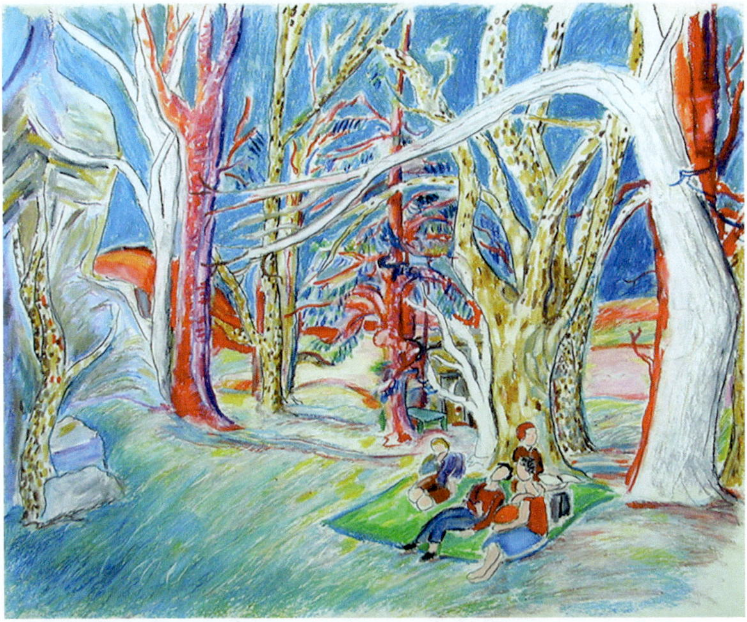

Figure 4.1: Priscilla, *Picnic*, early 1970s. Oil pastel and pencil on paper. 14 in. × 17 in. © Shaun McNiff.

responses to it sharply contrast with the psychopathology narratives and stigma pervading the discourse about art in mental health.

Anthony was one of the hospital artists featured in the exhibition. When we first met, he had not spoken for two decades and withdrew from human interaction after being admitted to a psychiatric hospital at the age of 15. In the studio sessions, he went from repeatedly making the same quick scribble drawing of a person (Figure 4.2) to responding to his environment with masterful drawings (Figure 4.3). The art, together with his verbal responses to it, offered convincing documentation of change, personal potential, artistic intelligence, and therapeutic efficacy (McNiff, 1972, 1974, 1975a). And in terms of the impact of art evidence on others, Anthony's artistic expression inspired me then and now, and helped provide a foundation for my lifework. Since his art has been widely viewed, I believe it has had a similar impact on many others.

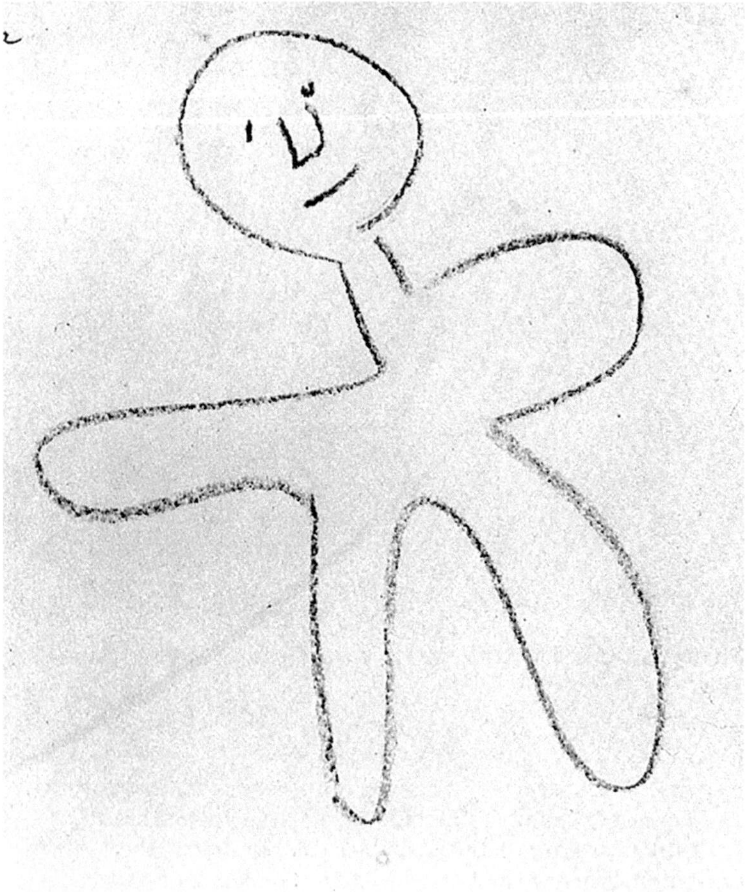

Figure 4.2: Anthony, *Quick Scribble*, ca. 1970. Pencil on paper. 9 in. × 12 in. © Shaun McNiff.

The empirical imagery is convincing. It does not require justification through attempts at translation into purported scientific formats far removed from its physical reality, all of which as stated above, overlook primary sources.

Furthermore, as the creator of the art evidence, Anthony's accomplishments are negated when they are not viewed as prima

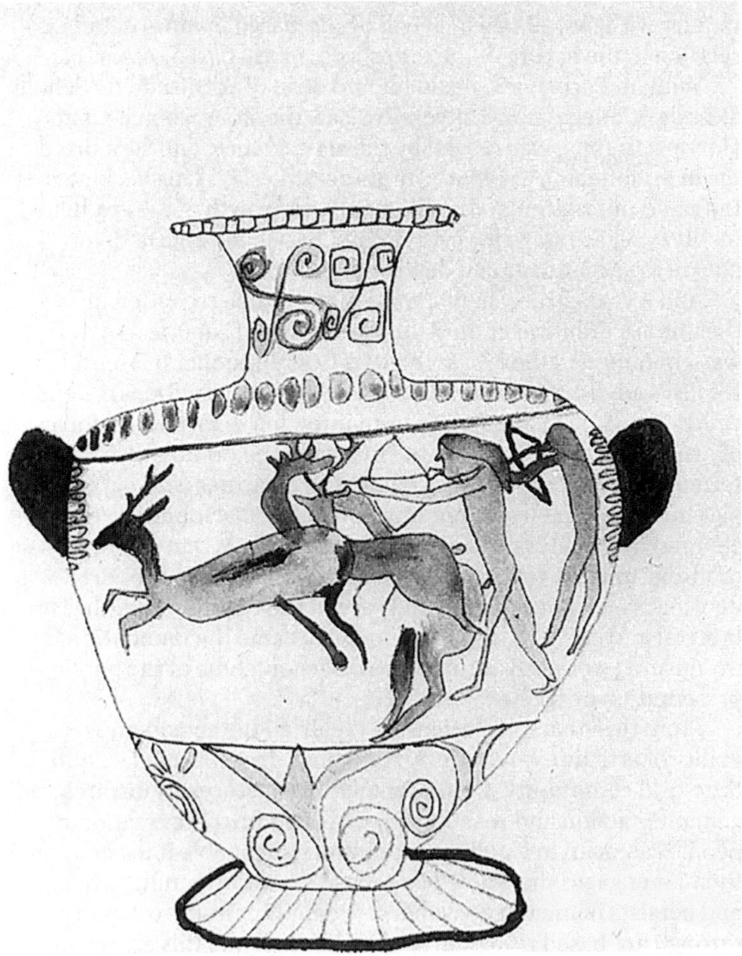

Figure 4.3: Anthony, *Vase*, ca. 1971. Pencil on paper. 9 in. × 12 in. © Shaun McNiff.

facie proof of his creative capabilities and his demonstration of how artistic expression can further personal change and well-being. In relation to the definition of art-based research, Anthony can be viewed as a principal actor in a cooperative artistic inquiry with me, all of which will be discussed in more detail in relation to the nature of the art process in art-based research.

William Perry, vice president and dean of the Graduate School at Lesley College (now University), saw the show when it visited Harvard in 1973, was moved by the art evidence, and supported me in establishing graduate programs at Lesley. This backing and the rapid international development and growth of the graduate institute set the stage for everything I have been able to do in advancing art and human development.

And a year earlier, in response to the public reception of the initial exhibition at the Addison Gallery of American Art, I was appointed to the Massachusetts Commissioner of Mental Health's advisory committee to represent what the Department called "expressive therapy," a term intended to include all forms of artistic expression. It was the first time the Commonwealth formally recognized and included art as a partner with psychiatry, psychology, social work, nursing, and other disciplines. We were charged by Commissioner William Goldman, MD to explore multidisciplinary training and staffing initiatives to support a new focus on community-based care in the Commonwealth. The integral and cross-disciplinary model became the foundation for my ensuing work. All of this was a direct outcome of the public presentation of art evidence.

From these early experiences, I realized the considerable ability of artistic expressions to influence decision-makers and the world community. Consistent with its history, art inspires and generates action and reaction, change, and furthers creation if people can open to its direct expression and enable it to act upon them. It engages the whole of a person's and community's being and persists in memory—which is yet another issue to explore through art-based research. And additionally, in this era when shared humanity is often overlooked, artistic expressions not only manifest inherent human qualities but also communicate across cultural differences. To achieve these effects, art evidence must be allowed to speak for itself, to naturally convey its creative energy and expression, and freely influence the people who engage it.

We strive to be more aware of and responsive to the artistic evidence carrying expression within its formal and aesthetic structures. As Hans-George Gadamer suggested, we try to "understand the phenomenon in its unique and historical concreteness" (Gadamer, 1994, p. 5) and create a relationship with it. The evidence is neutralized when it is not allowed to generate a new phase of its existence in communion with us.

The legal tradition's emphasis on the presentation of clear and convincing evidence is another practical principle that applies to art-based research. If we are to *make the case* that the artistic processes and outcomes generated by our research are evidence of efficacy, it follows that value will be influenced by the quality of the presentation. Quality matters in all forms of applied art practice and research—and in supporting egalitarian and universal accessibility, stereotypical notions of artistic quality and talent need to be replaced with more inclusive and credible standards.

I explore these issues in *Imagination in Action* (2015), emphasizing the innate tendency of an expression to manifest itself as effectively as possible, reframing quality as uniqueness and authenticity, while approaching artistic expression as a force of nature accessible to everyone. Does the expression convey creative energy, life, and impact others? And as Gadamer suggests, quality is also dependent on the ability of a person to perceive it, which we cannot control, but we can do our best to support the perceptions of others with clear and convincing evidence.

In my experience supervising research, considerable attention is given to how those conducting the inquiry select and curate what we describe as poignant artistic expressions from the extensive materials generated by the research process. This is especially significant when recording with video, where there tends to be copious footage, especially when we encourage comprehensive documentation of the artistic process. Editing becomes the core of research reflection, identifying outcomes, and choosing what to present. In the case of dissertations involving experimentation with research partners, editing, and creating concise video presentations of outcomes tend to become a primary form of artmaking in art-based research, all of which will be discussed in the forthcoming section dealing with video and new media.

My repeated support for concise presentations will hopefully not be taken as a disregard for epic poems, novels, films, and other expansive artistic expressions as well as the value of relaxed, extended, winding, and exploratory conversations in generating ideas. However, I have discovered through my own research experience and in supervising others, that brevity is best in relation to theses and dissertations. Extensive and wide-reaching investigations of issues related to research questions can contribute to inquiries that culminate in succinct, audience-friendly presentations in keeping with Robert Browning's: "Well, less is more, Lucrezia" (2024).

With art-based research, I look at the whole dissertation, thesis, or publication as an integral, coherent, and engaging work of art. I encourage advisees to write succinctly; in their own voices; quoting others only when necessary; clearly stating goals, methods, and outcomes; and always guided by efforts to engage and respect audiences, essentially in keeping with terse and convincing presentations of art evidence as suggested above. These artistic values of presentation can conflict with how academic and professional institutions require standardized formats, which will be explored in more depth in the following section.

The writing involved in doing and presenting art-based research, together with the more general organization of the text, is as much of an artistic creation and presentation as the more literal showing of what might be called art evidence—visual art, poetry and creative writing, video, soundtracks, and various modes of documenting dance, theatre, music, and other more temporal artistic expressions, and yet other art processes extending beyond the institutional forms. There is an ingrained assumption that the current jargon, concepts, and formats of social science are the exclusive methods for doing and communicating research. As I will discuss, these structural and linguistic forms are often not only expected but also mandatory, implying "procedure as a goal" (Potash, 2013, p. 53).

In keeping with Marshall McLuhan's "The medium is the message" (1964), fixed protocols reliably present themselves as the research outcomes, an ironic twist of the replication principles of science.

Although my own free experimentation with artistic inquiry, as described earlier, has not been constrained by these formats, in my role as a dissertation and thesis advisor in higher education, I have worked with my advisees to successfully complete their work within the institutional procedural requirements while maximizing every opportunity for artistic presentation. In *Art as Research* (2013), I affirm the artistic presentations of research theses emerging from the doctoral program at the Melbourne

Institute for Expressive and Creative Therapies (MIECAT) but in my experience, this artistic freedom is rare, and, in my view, it is a primary concern for the future as I will discuss.

David Orlinsky, a noted authority on psychotherapy research at the University of Chicago, has described current research as unreadable, "dull," redundant, humorless, and lacking depth in relation to the people described (2024). This observation is in sync with historian Hayden White's conviction that artistic qualities and imagination define classic and influential historical texts together with reason (1985, p. 123), and history needs to restore "an intimate connection with its literary base. ... In the interest of appearing scientific and objective, it has repressed and denied to itself its own greatest source of strength and renewal" (1985, p. 99). Orlinsky, committed to science, and White speaking for the humanities, seem to agree on the need for research processes and presentations having a creative and engaging "base."

Engaging art's unique presence and expression versus data analysis

Before closing this discussion of art evidence, it is important to stress that art-based research approaches artistic expressions as autonomous manifestations of the creative process.

As James Hillman, whom the poet Robert Bly described as, "the most lively and original psychologist we have had in America since William James" (1995, blurb) emphasized, the reduction of living things to concepts and typologies replaces uniqueness with "abstract emptiness" (1980, p. 26). He declared that "a field is its language" (1978, p. 203) and documented how the preponderance of "sterile," lifeless, and unimaginative language and textbook thinking permeates academic psychology and publishing.

In contrast, art-based research engages artistic expressions with the understanding that our experimentation is conducted in creative partnership with them and we do our best to artistically present the research process and outcomes so they can impact audiences and speak for themselves with integrity.

These core values are distinguished from the pervasive treatment of art in social and behavioral science research as inanimate "data," information, to be analyzed, processed, measured, and categorized, all of which echo the analytic reduction of a person's artistic expressions to dubious psychological concepts described earlier. Data generally consist of raw numbers and various forms of information that are collected and analyzed, interpreted, arranged, and presented in formats favoring statistical organization—tables, graphs, diagrams, etc.

While appreciating the importance of data analysis in many areas of inquiry, and as someone known throughout years of higher education leadership as "data driven" in relation to statistical and financial numbers relating to the total spectrum of organizational functions, I am not in any way challenging their place in various dimensions of life and science. The power and relevance of data in these areas, and especially now in the digital age, have generated an absolutism that all research in the human realm must involve the generation of data and its analysis as a primary focus and determinant of efficacy.[3] The blanket expectations, yet another attempt to reduce all research to science, have become so pervasive that my supervision of art-based research generally requires giving considerable attention to questioning language and methodological stereotypes.

The criticism of scientizing art processes is longstanding. Susanne K. Langer describes how "professionally approved language" and prescribed technical protocols "obscure phenomena" and impose "lines of thought" (1967, p. 36), highlighting how, "haste to become scientific destroys the most valuable material for investigation" (1967, p. 37). And Neil Postman, who as I mentioned earlier respected the natural sciences, decried scientism and the application of standardized measures to human experience where they do not apply: "We become fastidious about method only when one has no story to tell" (1984, p. 30). In contrast, artistic inquiry offers a renewal of imagination, its reality, and the ability to engage the full spectrum of life experiences. As Ursula Le Guin emphasized, art speaks the language of imagination and conveys its truth (1989) to those willing to explore its expression rather than projecting themselves and their analytic concepts and procedures onto it.

When engaging another person or groups of people, I do not approach them as data. As with all living things, they may share qualities together with inimitable characteristics and the same applies to the art that people make as I have emphasized as a fundamental quality of art-based research. In reflecting on the process of inquiry, we may identify patterns and continuities of human experience but do our best to appreciate and honor the individual *suchness* of artistic expressions, which cannot be reduced to conceptual categories.

They are not simply data to be analyzed but expressive entities that can inform and enhance experience. As with scientific research, we strive to carefully study and examine the art generated by the overall process of inquiry but differ from social science, and not necessarily the natural sciences, in approaching artistic actions and objects as living expressions and research partners. I will describe how art processes can also further reflection and interpretation of the overall research experience in the later discussion of practice.

Rudolf Arnheim's studies of the "direct and universal" (1974, p. 444) forces of expression structurally inherent to all forms of art offer guiding principles in engaging and perceiving it. He expands assumptions about the nature of artistic expression beyond exclusive identification with the thoughts and emotions of the persons who make the work, "the mind 'behind it'" (1974, p. 451) and affirms its expressive self-sufficiency. Psychology has almost exclusively analyzed art to determine what it says about the persons who create it, looking backwards in characteristically nebulous ways, overlooking how the analytic reductions say more about the biases and projections of the persons making the judgments.

Where the ethicist Emanuel Levinas opposed reducing the depth and complexity of the "other" to our thoughts and concepts (1969), the same can be applied to a person's art. Art therapy has historically been identified with this reductive direction in purporting to determine the underlying conditions of the persons who make art rather than looking forward in a comprehensive way to what the art process can do, how it can further well-being. What is the nature of the art's expression? How can we open to it as accurately as possible? How does it impact us? How can we further these processes through our ongoing responses and creative acts? And how do we present the outcomes?

On the receiving end, Arnheim demonstrates how artistic expressions generally present themselves to all people without preconditions. We relate to art through our sensory perceptions and imagination, just as we do with other living things. The traditions of art scholarship enrich the process of engagement and expand the exploration for those of us who wish to study them, but they, and even the statements of the artists themselves, are not the final and authoritative expositions of meaning that must stay open to unlimited and ongoing possibilities for relationship with others. Rather than assuming that expertise and pre-existing knowledge are needed to understand and relate to artworks, we can approach all of art as expressive entities that will have endlessly different relationships with the people who engage them in different moments in time. Picasso reportedly said that whenever he passed one of his paintings, they had a different conversation.

Arnheim viewed himself as a scholar grounded in both art and science who carefully observed what artists do and created methods of inquiry that strive to "enrich" the art rather than "avoiding" the whole of its presence (1974, pp. 8–9). Art's transmission "of life-giving energy" is not simply received but stimulates an endlessly variable and integrative "play of forces," involving the artistic expression and the persons who perceive it (1974, pp. 460–461). The ongoing relations create new life.

In my early work with art in a state mental hospital with chronic psychiatric patients, I consistently found how the perception of various art forms made during group sessions generated engagement, imaginative expression, and sensitive social interaction with otherwise withdrawn people who rarely spoke (1973).

We innately approached the artworks as "co-participants" offering their expression to every person involved in the process of engaging them. Within this open-ended invitation for relationship, those who made the art were affirmed when others related to it. And often participants expressed themselves more freely and imaginatively when responding to the art of other group members, perhaps because it presented a *tabula rasa* unrestricted by personal history. It was clear that each of us established our different ways of perceiving a particular work and that the possibilities for connection were manifold as in a lively conversation with another person. The artworks contributed to the group interaction.

These experiences, and others within the context of art-based research, can be viewed as building on the principle of art carrying expression conveyed by its physical structure. Within the conventional and reductive frameworks of art "analysis," there is an assumption that these qualities are amenable to a certain conceptual fixity. Our experimentation in the group studio suggests that empirical art expressions, while keeping a structural constancy in relation to perception, present endlessly varied interpretative and relational possibilities.

And within international training sessions over the last five decades, we have consistently experienced how the community of expression includes the art as well as the people who make it (Figure 4.4). The artistic expressions in various media are sources of creative contagion, fostering an overall atmosphere of imaginative possibilities and cooperation.

In 2018, I was invited to lead a London Art Therapy Centre gathering of 120 participants, organized by Hephzibah Kaplan and Gary Nash (Figure 4.5). The event was called *How art heals: Integrating practice and research.* My work has consistently focused on making art in community and groups, a process that generates a kinetic ecosystem of creative forces that influence participants and their art.

The London Art Therapy Centre created a nine-minute film documenting the studio workshop, available on the internet since 2018, that I consider an exemplary use of film in art-based

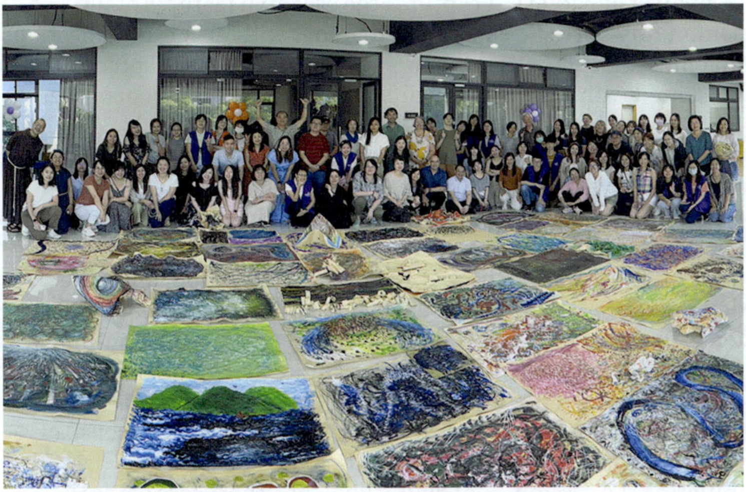

Figure 4.4: International Expressive Arts Therapy Association, Taiwan, 2023. Photo credit: Ted Johnson, MD.

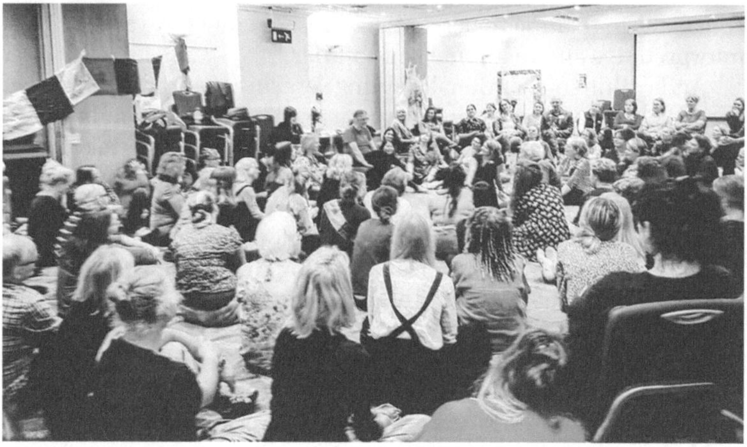

Figure 4.5: London Art Therapy Centre 1 with Marian Liebmann, OBE moving, 2018. Photo credit: Mirella Issaias.

research (https://arttherapycentre.com/galleries/video-howart-heals-integrating-practice-and-research-prof-shaun-mcniff/) (Kaplan et al., 2024). It captures the essential features of the community's artistic expression together with insightful reflections that illuminate how participants perceived the overall process, all presented with an artistic quality and precision that I encourage throughout this book.

The filmmaking team models the emphasis I place on video and film as vehicles for capturing the intricacies of creative action in particular moments in time and then engaging the editing process as a mode of artistic interpretation and shaping of the final artistic presentation. Among the many achievements of the film is the demonstration of the power of working collaboratively, which tends to characterize filmmaking. It also confirms the non-linear, community chemistry and environmental interplay of overt and subtle forces that do not lend themselves to linear analysis. Yet the film shows how the diverse elements cohere in a shared sense of purpose, much of which was not anticipated by me as the person initiating the session, confirming how the art process tends to improvise on our intentions and operate ahead of the reflecting mind.

It is important to mention that I had no involvement in planning, producing, shooting, and editing the film. However, since it documents a process of engaging a community of people in artistic expression in ways that have emerged from my practice over many years, I have considerable experience with the content being presented. I can report how the film gave me new perspectives on the work and strongly reinforced the potential of the medium in art-based research. This unplanned element and my lack of attachment to the making of the film add yet another dimension to its credibility.

In organizing the day, I had prepared to introduce the community to the movement basis of expression as a reliable and accessible way to make quality art in various media. I would make percussive rhythms, and the community would respond to them with visual art, practice witnessing one another working in pairs, interpret visual art with bodily movement and vocal enactment, all of which reinforce the integral relationship between the various senses in all forms of artistic expression.

In the morning session, we worked with simple black markers and conté crayons emphasizing how sustained elemental movement and gestures can shape dynamic images (Figures 4.6–4.8), and then responded to the art with spontaneous movement, rather than the more habitual talking and explanation. In my experience, the former tends to be more intimate and evocative of new insights, both when responding to our own art and witnessing partners move to their art and ours. The depth and originality of these spontaneous interpretations in various art media can be attributed to the absence of analytic and explanatory thinking and language. This art process, like so many others, suggests how artistic experimentation can further human understanding.

In the afternoon, participants made three-dimensional pieces with sticks and other objects from nature joined with twine and completed the day silently moving in a large circle to view each person's work.

In reflecting on their experience, group members affirmed the importance of practitioner research and, especially, their *firsthand* involvement with the processes that they hope to bring to others. After working alone within the community, they became more aware of the subtle qualities of another person's gestures when asked to select a partner and take turns witnessing one another

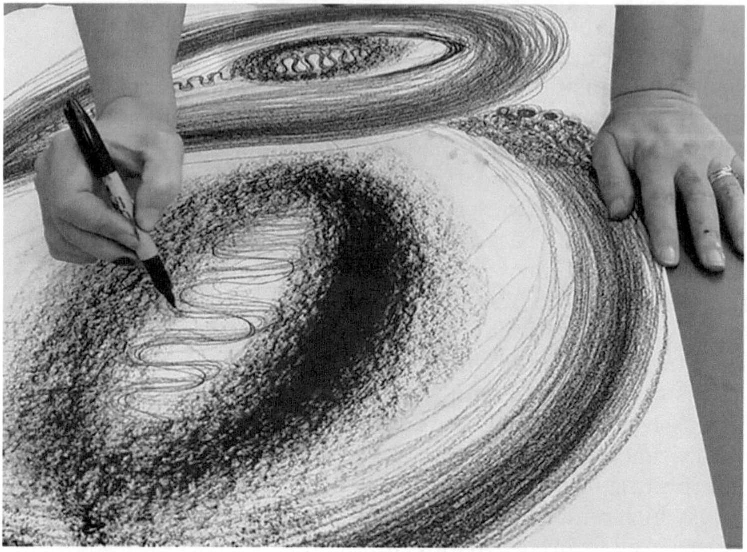

Figure 4.6: London Art Therapy Centre 2 with conté crayons and markers on paper, 2018. Photo credit: Mirella Issaias.

continue artmaking. Creating together in community affirmed how co-creation with others enhances and activates each person's individual expression as documented by the film and its art evidence.

Gabrielle Ereira, who offered to respond to her art through movement in a circle surrounded by the whole group, said: "It is letting go in safe place ... if I can't do that, how can I expect other people to do it?" (Kaplan et al., 2024).

The film offers succinct artistic impressions and selections from a complete day of community participation, fashioned into an integral work of art. Even though the multiple cameras capture what might be considered empirical actions and images, they clearly reflect individual perspectives in time and place as I will emphasize in a later discussion of video. This distillation of what the filmmakers considered to be essential features of the group experience generated a new work of art, and what I am describing here as art evidence that expresses itself and acts upon those

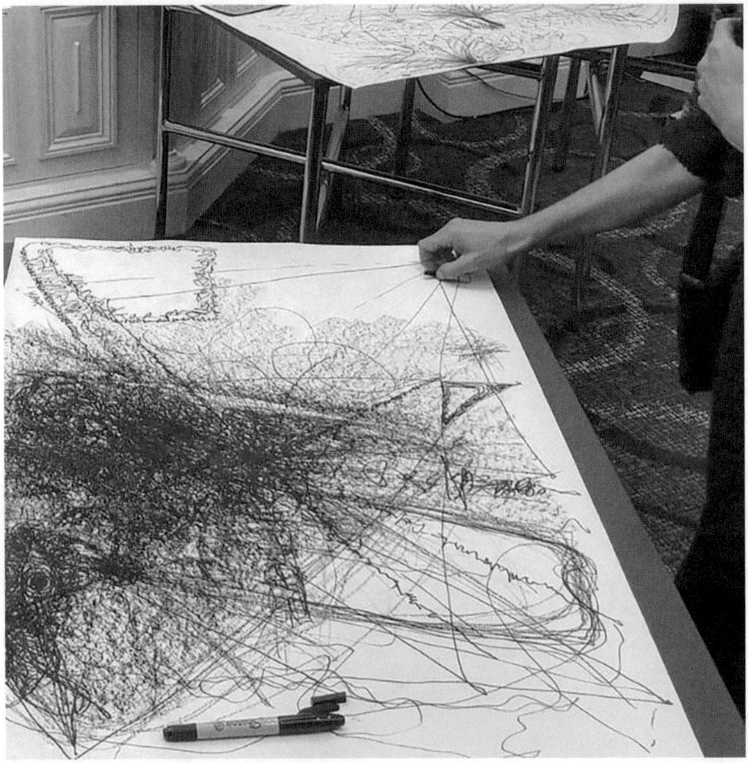

Figure 4.7: London Art Therapy Centre 3 with conté crayons and markers on paper, 2018. Photo credit: Mirella Issaias.

who view it. The film does not simply record and replicate what presents itself to the camera. It creates life.[4]

As I have demonstrated, our interpretations and personal responses are varied. Although the film presents a coherent and accurate overview of the day's activity, it does not show the innumerable sensibilities and acts of the whole group of participants. And as I will demonstrate later, even when recording the close-up actions of one person, the recording process always presents a selective point of view on the action. The artistic framing of action heightens and concentrates reality rather than diminishing it.

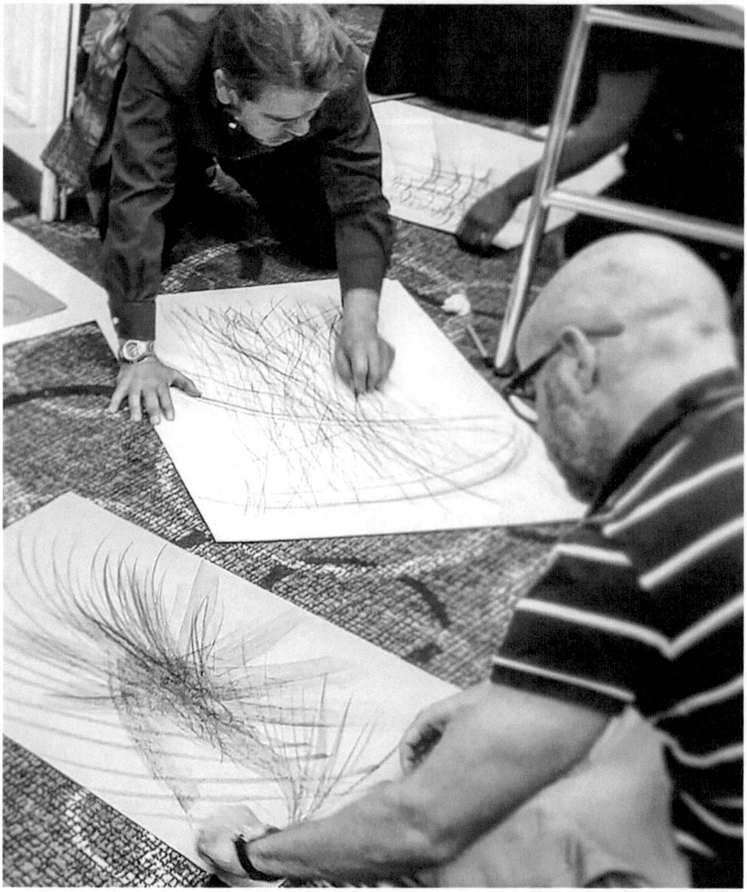

Figure 4.8: London Art Therapy Centre 4 with conté crayons and markers on paper, 2018. Photo credit: Mirella Issaias.

The film presents what its makers record and compose. It cannot show the multifarious, often invisible, and uncatchable intricacies of what each person experiences. This is consistent with the perception of experience, suggesting an honest presentation. The medium offers an observation of a life event in a meticulously empirical, factual, and engaging form. It is thoroughly unscripted *cinema verité*. Can we get any closer to reality? As I will discuss later, even though this description emphasizing observed fact fits the common definition of objectivity, the realization of an unconditionally objective viewpoint, untouched by the influence of perception, is illusory.

Of course, the artistry of the film and the creative synthesis it creates influence the viewers' perceptions of the work. But rather than distorting, it arguably enhances awareness with its clarity and craft as contrasted to the obscuring effects of less proficient presentations. As I emphasize throughout this book, and while supporting universal accessibility of art-based research, quality presentation furthers engagement and impact as it has done in all forms of research throughout history (White, 1985).

We can ask, what does the film as research offer in relation to furthering understanding? How might it compare to processes generating *data* to be *analyzed* in responses to the community event—i.e., the pervasive social science surveys, questionnaires, and other mathematically scorable assessments that could be completed by the 120 participants?

Clearly, surveys can be useful and efficient in straightforward evaluations of experiences. For example, when I was helping the Dana-Farber Cancer Institute in Boston with the implementation of art programs for patients and family members, I encouraged a brief questionnaire asking for direct assessments of value and satisfaction on a 1-to-5, low-to-high scale—with a primary emphasis on feelings before and after art sessions. The materials were useful in affirming the program and identifying strengths, together with areas for adjustment and change.

As a person whose teaching, advising, lecturing, leadership, and professional practice have been evaluated systematically by surveys for over five decades, and who has reviewed the evaluation data of many hundreds of faculty members and other academics as a dean and provost, the processes clearly have a fundamental and necessary role in assessing and improving performance. Without getting into detail with this expansive subject, I can simply say that in my experience of being evaluated by data collected and scored by these instruments, the procedure has accurately identified strengths and weaknesses in my work with others, and it has significantly helped improve and affirm practice. Similarly, my engagement with others in the assessment of their work has consistently shown the same value when people are open to it. The primary outcome of this experience is that the instruments, when designed with consensual criteria, document satisfaction and dissatisfaction of participants and generate important *data* for people and institutions striving to be effective in addressing the needs of others. As much as I agree with William James saying in 1887 that when it comes to understanding complex human experience, a single insightful person "carefully cross-examined, is more likely to deepen our knowledge than a thousand circulars [questionnaires] as the average person answers them" (2025), there is clearly a place for surveys. Statistical assessments tend to collect and illuminate opinion, ironically built upon subjective judgments enclosed in certain moments in time. They have their place but do not necessarily address the deepening of understanding and enrichment of experience suggested by William James. The London film, as an illustration of the extensive art-based research I have experienced and envision for the future, expands possibilities beyond itself, invites participation and experimentation, furthers imagination, and illustrates how to document and artistically present art evidence while respecting and suggesting uncatchable infinities moving with us, then and now.

The way we engage, think about, and talk about the art generated in our research, and artistically present it, are distinguishing features of the art-based research community. We creatively and sensitively respond to artistic expressions, animate them with our attention, and do our best to open to what they offer through an interactive process of interpretation.

Notes

1. The 2019 Netflix documentary series, *Happy Jail*, directed by Michele Josue and produced and edited by Liam McNiff, explores life within the CPDRC prison and offers another illustration of artistic inquiry. For reference, see p. 67.
2. A comprehensive collection of the art can be viewed on the Danvers State Hospital historical website created by John Gray (2024). https://www.danversstatehospital.org/art-therapy. See p. 68.
3. Taken to new extremes with today's increasing reliance on programmed technologies determining value through the bibliometric counting of citations, all far removed from Arnheim's references to "the smell of the studio" and "genuine human

expression" and prone to widely reported manipulation and ethical misuse. See p. 76.

4. In his book *Film as Art* (originally written in Germany as *Film als Kunst*, later translated into English by M. Sieveking and Ian F. D. Morrow, and first published in London in 1933 by Faber and Faber), Arnheim emphasizes how the art form of film does not present a "mechanical reproduction of reality." Rather than imitating life, art transforms what is experienced and perceived into new and self-sufficient forms (1957, p. 3), a new reality. See p. 83.

5 Doing Art-Based Research in Academic Settings

One person's perspective

I cannot emphasize enough that the following discussion is informed largely by my experience, one person's interpretation of the issues, albeit informed by over five decades of supervising and reviewing the academic research of students and colleagues working together to further artistic inquiry. As Jerome Kagan, the eminent developmental psychologist at Harvard University, said when I met with him in the mid-1970s: "There are no absolutes in psychology," and this principle applies to doing art-based research as I describe it here. I continuously discover different approaches to, and instances of, artistic inquiry, and I trust that this will continue in keeping with art's perpetual uniqueness and reliable creation of new and unpredictable contributions within an ideally open research environment.

Also, as to how this reflection on practice might influence research, I see it as a collegial discussion of my experience with a relatively new approach to research in higher education. It is neither a procedural manual nor a presentation of models to be used. As I have mentioned earlier, art is infinitely variable, but we carefully study what other artists do, and have done, in a larger sphere of influences and inspirations. C. G. Jung, whom I admire and whose *Liber Novus* as mentioned earlier is exemplary art-based research, famously gave thanks for not being a Jungian. For example, rather than attempting to replicate or systematize what Jung did, I encourage being like him in creating your approaches to artistic inquiry, all echoing William Blake's exhortation in *Jerusalem* to "create a system" rather than be limited to what others have done.

Since my work in relation to art-based research has been presented in the public sphere, I am often asked for guidance by students who hope to generate dissertations and theses through artistic inquiry. The need for practical counsel as to how artistic processes can inform research, is the stimulus for this book, where I can hopefully offer an in-depth discussion of what I have learned—what I recommend based on these experiences, perceptions of what has worked, what has not, what might be perfected in the future, and most of all, what I consider to be the issues, needs, challenges, and opportunities that transcend my experience and possibly apply to more general practice.

Whatever is presented here that might have value and resonance will hopefully help to inform the discourse between students conducting research and their advisors, the "co-creative process," which is the crux of academic research formation and direction. When I am asked for help with initiating art-based research projects, I keep deferring to the advising relationship as the place for engaging subtleties and complexities of research, and thus my respect for organizations and academic disciplines that defer to it.

My experience informing the following discussion and recommendations has been, as previously described, largely within the applied art realm cooperating with health, education, and psychology.[1] Therefore, I have considerable experience dealing with expectations that formal research will follow social scientific formats and procedures. I will explore how we developed art-based research within this specific, and sometimes restrictive, context. The process of making the case for a distinctly different alternative to a dominant paradigm has hopefully furthered the development of clear and convincing approaches for the future.

It is my wish that in addition to addressing issues of concern for those working in the applied art areas where there is considerable interest in art-based research, the material presented will be useful in furthering the more expansive use of artistic understanding as I have continuously encouraged (2013). I believe the fundamental principles cross disciplinary lines and my aspirations have always been concerned with the most comprehensive integration of artistic inquiry with the fullness of life, again as a complement, and not in any way as a challenge to science.

Since the scope of art is vast, it is my hope that this discussion of art-based research, emerging from a particular area of practice, can be a bridge to others. Ideally, the microspheres within specific disciplines suggest points of correspondence with the whole of art.

Working within limits and prescribed formats

In beginning a discussion dealing with practical issues related to doing and supervising art-based research within academic institutions, I address my experience as a doctoral advisor within the common situation where format requirements and their underlying paradigms do not completely align with artistic inquiry and presentation. I start with this challenge because the tension is pervasive in the applied art area and must be addressed first, to navigate the existing conditions and requirements, but also to use the experience to identify shared principles likely to be encountered in other disciplines. Although I do not support mandatory and uniform formats that prejudice a prevailing academic scientism, with their echoes of the *Procrustean rule*, I have learned a great deal working within them, which I believe can apply to all forms of artistic inquiry in higher education.

Universities and their libraries, as well as most professional publications, tend to require standard textual styles and formats—APA, MLA, Chicago, Harvard, etc. There are many practical reasons for textual consistency within institutions, which are not questioned here. Most of my academic supervision has involved the use of the American Psychological Association (APA) style and formats. My experience with APA-required formatting has generally been helpful in terms of its contributions to consistency, clarity, and accessibility.

Although the mandatory use of IMRaD formatting (Introduction, Methods, Results, and Discussion, as derived from scientific studies) is not an official APA requirement, it is often required or assumed (Atkins, 2012), as in the program where I have supervised a considerable amount of art-based research. The compulsory use of IMRaD for the presentation of art-based research is a scientization of artistic inquiry and antithetical to it, but we have adapted, and it has ironically helped in some ways to further clarity and concision, as I will describe.

However, I unequivocally support format freedom and flexibility in relation to the more general practice of art-based and all other forms of research, where formats can ideally respond to the nature of a study. This contrasts with how uniformities impose ways of thinking, organization, and appearance, as suggested above by Susanne K. Langer.

As I try to show in the following pages, direct and engaging writing, all permeated by the voice of the writer, are qualities I encourage. The text is approached as an integral element of the overall artistic presentation, illuminating and supporting other forms of art evidence. This principle is yet another example of safeguarding the human presence as the world embraces artificial and machine-generated language. Brevity, in my experience, is consistently challenging. I have reviewed art-based dissertations that go on for several hundred pages and yet more in appendices. The discipline of expository writing encourages an integration of necessary content and getting to the point with as much precision as possible. Reading dissertations and theses over many years has reinforced this inclination.

To the extent that IMRaD furthers articulation of essential points and limits tangential discussions, it has been helpful, especially in how it models clear framing of research questions and issues, and the empirical methods to be used in exploring them before presenting the research process and outcomes. If we are to realize format freedom with art-based research, hopefully lessons learned from IMRaD will be sustained.

In my advising relationships, I embrace the concrete who, what, when, and where aspects of research methodology, as I will discuss later in detail together with the presentation of art-based research and core outcomes. But first, we give close attention to the "why" in formulating research questions in terse and uncomplicated language. This emphasis on "questions," as with IMRaD, can also be posed as exploring "issues, problems, and so forth." For our purposes here and to further simplicity, I will refer to all these possibilities as questions.

Regarding the use of required structures in art-based research, I again appreciate the general orientation within an academic institution toward consistent styles and formats for the presentation of final manuscripts and their submission to university libraries. Regarding APA, it is a system with an emphasis on concision and clarity that has been tested and perfected over many years with millions of participants and consequently conveys considerable wisdom to be applied in domains outside the social sciences. My experience with it has been positive. I am sure the same applies to the use of MLA, Chicago, Harvard, and other widely used and tested styles.

However, with the presentation of art-based research, there should be flexibility and creativity regarding the inclusion of art evidence and other design features that support artistic presentation and discourse. Format freedom, as I emphasized decades ago (1986a), is an inherent and ideally defining feature of artistic inquiry as contrasted to standardization; therefore, it is appropriate to maintain a certain degree of creative tension between the mutually valid concerns of consistency and artistic presentation. Hopefully, in this era when university libraries are digitizing dissertations and theses rather than the traditional shelving of bound manuscripts, they can increasingly accommodate artistic presentation and design.

Where, as I have described, the uniformity of the IMRaD format created to present scientific research, has helped to shape approaches to dissertation writing that can be applied to art-based research, it should not be mandatory. The format *structure* can easily become a *stricture*, especially since the standardization of form contradicts the nature of art. Rather, I suggest carefully studying the various formats, their histories, and principles, with the goal of determining how they might be of use in guiding the presentation of research. Ultimately, all approaches to dissertation writing and presentation can inform one another. My experience affirms a cross-disciplinary understanding of their various features and then encouraging the use of whatever structure and style best serve the purpose and most effective communication of the research.

Breadth of artistic possibilities

When considering the prospect of doing formal art-based research within an academic environment, I encourage envisioning a research question or direction, what art form or forms might be used, and how the work might be presented. Ultimately, the structure of the research and the content inform one another. In some cases, these issues and intentions might have already emerged organically in personal artistic experimentation as I have documented through my history. Often, as I will discuss, the research direction is not yet clear, and open-ended artistic exploration can further its emergence. Ideally, this envisioning is not encumbered by mandatory format requirements, and it can be pursued with artistic freedom.

Perhaps there are two fundamental and consistent qualities of all art-based research: Their infinite variability in terms of the art forms, methods of inquiry, and outcomes, and the use of art to conduct and present the research. In my community of practice, colleagues have consistently demonstrated the breadth of possibilities.

One of my first exposures to artistic inquiry came through a collaboration with Robert Coles in the mid-1970s. Although the term *art-based research* has not been applied to his 1973 Pulitzer Prize in General Nonfiction for Volumes II and III of the five-volume *Children of Crisis* series, which furthered major advances within the civil rights movement of the 1960s and 1970s, it is an exemplary demonstration of the time-tested use of art to further human understanding. And in addition to his writing, Robert Coles made drawings together with children and recorded their stories in response to them in a comprehensive research process (McNiff & Coles, 1976.)

Also, in the discipline of creative writing, my mentor, the historical novelist Truman Nelson, insisted that imaginal reality enabled him to go deeper than a literal account of the past. He said: "There is an overruling psychological truth that can come out of my absorption of the total empirical substance that I am transmitting" (Schafer, 1989, p. 276).

And through my colleagues I discovered Charlotte Salomon (1917–1943), whose *Leben oder Theater?* [*Life or Theater?*] (1981), created between 1941 and 1943 before her life was taken in Auschwitz, once again demonstrates the extraordinary depth and truth, in keeping with Truman Nelson's definition,[2] presented through art. The 769 paintings and accompanying text comprising her autobiographical play constitute one of the great moments in art history, illuminating the depth and influence of artistic inquiry authentically crafted from the conditions of a person's life.

The work of Charlotte's mentor, Alfred Wolfsohn (1896–1962), the German singing teacher who developed methods of vocal expression through his personal immersion in the medium, can be considered another major illustration of art-based inquiry and likened to C. G. Jung's *Liber Novus*.

While serving as a stretcher bearer during World War I, Wolfsohn is reported to have experienced shock and hallucinations from his exposure to shelling and the screams of wounded and dying soldiers. Hospitalization and psychiatric treatment were not effective, and he turned to his own exploration of the range of uninhibited vocalization, including the expression of extreme sounds, the soul *in extremis*.

His artistic inquiry led to establishing a Voice Research Center in Berlin, reconstituted during World War II in London. Wolfsohn's work is sustained by the Roy Hart Theatre in France (now the Centre Artistique International Roy Hart), Paul Newham (1993, 1998), Anne Brownell et al. (2024), Lena Måndotter (2024), and others. The Wolfsohn tradition maintains his original discipline of continuous and in-depth personal artistic experimentation and inquiry as the foundation of training and practice rather than morphing into a conceptual system. It serves as a model and inspiration for furthering well-being and human understanding through art.

These examples suggest the depth and range of possible inquiries, the various art forms they may involve, the realities conveyed, and their shared purpose in what D. H. Lawrence described as *transmitting life* and affirming it.

Other colleagues offer examples of possibilities for ongoing artistic experimentation and research.

In his book *Teaching Actors* (2012), Ross W. Prior shows how theatre has sustained participatory artistic inquiry and experimentation. The ensemble creates and learns through their shared experience and cooperation in settings commonly called actors' workshops.

Mitchell Kossak's focus on empathetic attunement and mis-attunement, when working with all forms of artistic expression in therapy, extends directly from his personal music practice (2008, 2021).

As mentioned earlier, Barbara Fish and Gary Nash have expanded and deepened the use of art in therapy with their research exploring reflection upon practice with others through personal artistic expression.

The poet Elizabeth Gordon McKim's exploration of relationships between poetry, body movement, and the full range of voice and vocalization in singing and chanting poems is closely attuned to my commitments to understanding and perfecting the use of multiple and complementary art forms. It might be asked, how do these bodily and vocal expressions influence the delivery and experience of a poem from the perspective of the poet? How do they affect audiences? How do they compare to the traditional reading of poetry? Experiencing words on a page?

I have been intrigued for decades with how Margo Fuchs Knill gives feedback to the creations of students in poems and drawings. A study might explore how those receiving artistic responses react to them. How does the experience compare to more conventional speech? Are there distinct differences between the two? What are they? In expanding Elizabeth's voice and movement dimensions, we can ask: How might singing/chanting the poetic response, or singing and moving with it, influence the impact? The same questions can be posed to those giving artistic feedback.

Regarding chanting, it might be asked how sustained vocal repetition of essential words influences the effect on the person receiving the response? The person giving it? In my studios, I find that most people need support in slowing their speech when reading a poem to feel and clearly enunciate the words rather than saying them in a more automatic way. I have discovered that repeated reading of brief poems while varying emphasis on passages helps people become more physically and emotionally united with their poetic expressions, consistent with the earlier mention of Klaus Boegel's research with performance art.

Sister Katheleen Burke researched the life and work of Hildegard of Bingen, with a special emphasis on her concept and practice of "greening," *viriditas*. I can imagine Sr. Kathleen painting spontaneously with her watercolors while meditating on the life and work of Hildegard. Does this contemplation influence her art? How? When doing this both indoors in a studio and outside in a natural environment, are there differences? Is one "greener" than the other?

In my studio groups, as demonstrated in *Art as Medicine* (1992), we explore responding to artworks in various forms of artistic expression as contrasted to the exclusive use of verbal descriptions and narratives as described earlier. This process of responding to art with art, by the person creating the piece and/or by other group members and then comparing the processes and outcomes to more common narrative explanations can generate extensive variations of research since there are so many potential relationships among the different art forms—for example, responding to a painting with movement, vocal improvisation, performance, brief poetic passages, etc., and the same can be done by shifting the relationships between art forms by interpreting and responding to a poem with visual art, movement, performance, etc.

Any one of these possibilities can be developed into an art-based research dissertation exploring simple questions regarding the accuracy, imagination, generative possibilities, satisfaction, and overall impact of responding artistically to a person's art, and how this can be contrasted to more conventional spoken comments and affirmations.

In my studios, two group members will often work together in responding through movement to their own visual art and the work of their partner. One person will give the movement interpretation, and the other will silently witness as described earlier in relation to the London Art Therapy Centre session. Participants consistently describe how they experience greater intimacy and depth when responding to another person's art. They express, as mentioned earlier, that it offers a *tabula rasa* as contrasted to the history and preconceptions often attached to their own work.

A student in a graduate training studio said she can respond with immediacy in the present moment when relating to another person's art—"I go with what I am seeing and feeling which is harder to do with my own work." These experiences raise the question of how we can bring the same spontaneity and directness to interactions with our own art; how we might let go of attachments and approach the work as if we are perceiving it for the first time.

Participants also describe how the presence of a supportive partner, acting as a witness, brings a sense of sanctity rather than judgment. As I hope to demonstrate in the coming section on simplicity and focus, the depth of artistic inquiry, in my experience, tends to correspond to a comprehensive exploration of a particular facet of a greater whole. This concentration will in turn enhance insight into the larger realm and the many ways of engaging it.

Having been educated in the discipline of history, I feel that this mode of inquiry can take on major significance within art-based research committed to improving practice using video and film. Video and film, perhaps more than any other medium, can turn the tables on the ingrained and static formalities of academic research dealing with human experience. In addition to preserving formative work, the medium documents practice, live action, and reflection on it, all of which in turn invite further reflection and response.

Bruce Moon's use of film to explore the work of individual contributors to art therapy is an exemplary manifestation of art-based research that suggests and inspires many future possibilities, as I will discuss in relation to the use of new media. His work is included in the historical and educational film library dealing with the creative arts therapy disciplines, *Expressive Media, Inc.*, established in 1985 by Judith Rubin and Eleanor Irwin (2024).

Bruce often describes how when he was first introduced to art therapy, his mentor Don Jones asked him to keep a sketchbook nearby, not necessarily to record what took place during sessions but for his artistic responses to them (2010). Moon has sustained this practice and expanded it by composing and performing music, poetry, and storytelling often with video documentation of the process, all constituting a comprehensive and widely presented body of art-based research.

Another close colleague, Norma Canner (1918–2012), was the first faculty member I recruited when establishing Lesley graduate programs. With her background in theatre, dance, and working with children with multiple disabilities, she modeled the integration of all art forms for me, faculty, and students (Figure 5.1). Her lifework is documented in an award-winning film (Brownell & Wilcoxen, 1998) that I believe unequivocally demonstrates the imperative to research art with art if we are to create convincing and inspirational presentations of the "evidence."

In speaking to me about the process of creating his iconic photograph of Norma in action, Barry Sugarman—who was advising master's thesis students at the time—reinforced the above-mentioned principle of empathetic attunement emphasized by Mitchell Kossak. He describes how the quality of photographs responding to other people is influenced by his immersion in the present moment of their expression (personal communication, September 9, 2025).

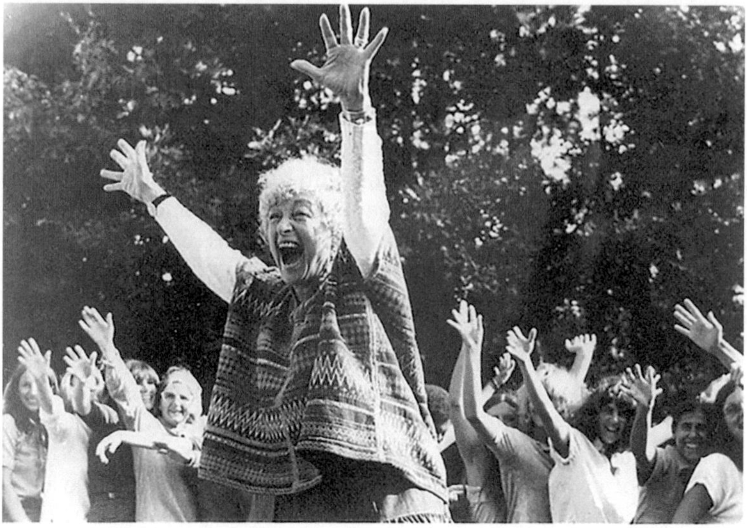

Figure 5.1: Norma Canner, group dance, 1982. Photo credit: Barry Sugarman.

And more recently, Gloria Simoneaux (2025) and her colleagues in the long-standing project, Harambee Arts, in Nairobi Kenya, have documented their work with a short film, *Ambassadors of Hope* (https://www.harambeearts.org/), that won the 2024 Dan Eldon Activist Award. In 2008, Gloria was a Fulbright Fellow at the University of Nairobi, which led to the creation of the project—*Harambee* is a Swahili word for "Let's pull together." She is now completing another film presenting the work of Harambee Arts in Nepal in cooperation with a Kathmandu organization dealing with human trafficking and forced prostitution.

Since filmmakers, especially in the documentary genre like the previously mentioned Frederick Wiseman, tend to do sophisticated and impactful research, they strengthen the case for designing academic research structures and modes of presentation that fit the content and process of the inquiry. And for me personally, the film series *Country Music* created by Ken Burns (2019), offering historical documentation of how this art form emerged and was influenced by various sectors of American culture, has been a major learning experience.

Are these important forms of artistic inquiry, which do not correspond to formats such as IMRaD, to be considered outside the domain of sanctioned research? Or is it past time for institutional research to align itself more completely with reality and the full range of human expression and communication?

In offering this panoply of art-based research possibilities, a small fraction from just my experience, I am trying to show the great range of potential projects, which in turn will hopefully further support for organizational formats and modes of presentation that highlight and maximize their impact.

Freedom of inquiry

It is reasonable to ask whether opening to the breadth of art in research, together with format freedom, will undermine order, academic discipline, and the assessment of quality. For example, Helen Frankenthaler's insistence that there can be "no rules" in making art[3] can be viewed as contrary to the core academic enterprise and evoke prospects of chaos. In addressing the issue of rules in art, it is important to acknowledge the formative forces of disruption in both art and science.

Openness and the absence of prescribed structure can generate a certain degree of uncertainty, but this is, as I have mentioned earlier, a reliable feature of artistic discovery. If there is a *rule* possibly consistent with Frankenthaler's statement about the art process, it may be that its depth requires willingness to engage the unknown, persist in the challenging work, and trust its ability to help us establish a direction.

Although I agree with the general avoidance of prescriptive rules in relation to art and the complete creative process, especially as I will discuss in relation to natural art experiments corresponding closely to the making of art, there are principles and standards inherent to artistic expression. Putting aside all the societal notions and stereotypes regarding artistic quality, I have emphasized how within the most basic gestures and movements of artmaking there tends to be an inherent force seeking the most effective expression (2015). And artists, in all forms of creation, while embracing uncertainty and not knowing as conditions for discovery, are driven by the urge and goal of "getting it right."

Art involves a fundamental perfecting process and discipline that happens within the context of the immediate creation. I have always preferred to simply ask: Does it work? In addition to asking this to myself in response to what I create, I ask others whose perceptions I trust and respect. In art-based research, these ongoing assessments permeate the inquiry and guide the creation of the final presentation.

Notes

1. Reference to art is again inclusive of all forms of artistic expression and not just the visual arts. For reference, see p. 89.
2. Nelson's sense of truth concurs with Hans-Georg Gadamer, who felt that it involves an experience or event that transforms or changes us. While respecting science, Gadamer opposed the all-encompassing use of the scientific method to reduce life processes to its circumscribed measures (1994). See p. 93.
3. "There are no rules ... that is how art is born, that is how breakthroughs happen. Go against the rules or ignore the rules, that is what invention is about" (Frankenthaler, 2024). See p. 99.

6

Research Structure: Simpler the Deeper

The following reflections on expository writing qualities and structures address ideas and recommendations that I view as general principles applying to the breadth of art as research and the spectrum of possibilities I encourage. Most of the issues discussed can also relate to all forms of academic research and not just artistic inquiry.

Concise, jargon-free, and natural writing

As emphasized throughout this book, one of my major learning experiences from decades of experience with academic research is the importance of concise writing. Communicating complex phenomena simply and directly in jargon-free and direct prose is one of the most challenging aspects of the research process. The accessibility and impact of the research will depend upon the ability to do this and effectively integrate the extensive information, materials, and art generated by the study. Current academic and professional research within the social sciences is permeated with often unintelligible jargon and its accompanying concepts, and the same can sometimes be the case today within the humanities.

I have found that writing in the first person, versus the faceless and soulless third person, "the researcher," and in one's natural voice, tends to further readability. As Miles Davis said, it can take a long time "to play like yourself" (2024), and I see this as a never-ending objective in my work. Staying grounded in oneself can deter the excessive tangents, citing, quoting, and coverage of everything possibly related to the research, often characterizing academic writing. Avoiding extraneous references to things other than the immediate and empirical process of the artistic inquiry will also support the integrity of the writing process. Writing composed in the voice of the person doing the research and focused on the distinctive features of the artistic inquiry will guard against the possibility of failing to acknowledge the work of others or inadvertently presenting another's language as one's own, which is unfortunately widespread today and being disclosed with the assistance of digital technology.

There is a general tendency in dissertation writing to believe that the quantity of pages will impact the quality and the credibility of the research. In my experience, excess has been a major deterrent. I realize that dissertations and theses entail considerable content to be presented, and that writers can become closely attached to it, but I have found that an emphasis on concision furthers an effort to strike the right balance and cohesion of the whole.

Literature and citing

I appreciate how psychological writing guides stress terse and precise presentations; avoidance of quotes, and especially long ones; condensing the ideas and statements of others and presenting them in your own voice rather than paraphrasing; and accurately referencing sources. However, I am flexible on quoting, especially when a passage may clarify, affirm, and speak to the core issues of a study. But I encourage judicious use, only when enhancing a position or clearly articulating what is questioned or opposed.

While categorically reinforcing the importance of acknowledging and attributing the works and ideas expressed by others, and I have done my share in this manuscript, there is a tendency in social science research and writing to cite excessively rather than communicate in natural and jargon-free language. My advisees are encouraged to avoid what I call *cite-itis* and *hyper-citing*, which can result in an academically officious, overly dense, and tedious text, while also detracting from where citations are essential to support positions, identify sources, and support further exploration of ideas.

I encourage doctoral dissertation writers to do their best to locate cites and essential quotes primarily in text examining the research and ideas of others, such as the IMRaD Literature Review or the Discussion area, where study outcomes are compared to what others have done. And when citing, highlight seminal works and others that relate directly to the research being presented. I suggest avoiding citations altogether when presenting the research itself and when describing questions, methods, and outcomes. They tend to obscure focus on the immediate work and the presentation of reflections on the process and outcomes.

These issues related to citing lead to the larger matter of dealing with literature and the works of others. Since the pertinent literature related to an inquiry can be vast, I have always recommended selective curating rather than comprehensive coverage, which can become overwhelming in its scope and density while obstructing concentration on works essential to the research. In my early thesis writing, Rudolf Arnheim encouraged me to mention the work of those who inform my positions and those with whom I disagree. He felt this approach sharpened the focus and offered a more engaging dialectic for the reader.

My general perception of the many dissertations I have reviewed in the social science and applied art areas is that literature reviews are unnecessarily long. I appreciate efforts to be thorough but ultimately precision and reader engagement are furthered through concision, which as Cicero and many others describe as taking considerably more time,[1] and I think discipline.

The IMRaD format, as previously described, deals with the work of others in the Literature Review after the Introduction, and in the Discussion section, where research outcomes are related to the preceding presentation of literature. Looking at the broader landscape of what has been done in relation to a research project makes sense at the beginning. It furthers a terse introduction and presents the context for the work. In discussing format freedom in *Art-Based Research* (1998a), I considered how too much emphasis on previous work at the start could prejudice the ensuing description of the research and suggested that a presentation of literature, and how the research relates to what others have done could be included as a closing section, as with the IMRaD Discussion chapter. This concern, raised years ago, was responding to the common practice of writing lengthy and often dense reviews of literature, as opposed to concise presentations as recommended here, before beginning to discuss the actual research process.

Ultimately, and in relation to art-based research, I think a review of influential literature and its relationship to the research is an important part of a dissertation or thesis. In accordance with the earlier discussion of format freedom, those doing and supervising the research can be empowered to make decisions as to its most effective placement and use within the text.

Abstracting and distilling

I have grown to appreciate abstracts at the beginning of dissertations, both as an encapsulation of the whole but also as models for identifying and communicating the essential features throughout the text. When encouraging succinct and uncomplicated presentation of research outcomes with my advisees, I say—imagine you have two or three minutes to convey your research to a person or audience you want to engage, and use this scenario to practice articulating your study as you will do in your abstract. This consolidation can then become the structure for the more comprehensive reflection on the significance of the work and the presentation of art evidence generated by the research.

As a reader of dissertations, I often find myself searching through copious pages trying to find terse and clear statements of research questions and outcomes. In addition to helping readers understand the research, the process of distilling (McNiff, 1998b, pp. 100–108) the essence of the work supports the articulation of its significance. In keeping with the adage, if we cannot describe a situation tersely and simply, we do not understand it.

In this sense, abstracting, or distilling, is a process that is sustained throughout the whole research experience and contrasts with defining abstraction as immateriality and non-concreteness. Abstracting is not just concerned with conceptual language, but also thoroughly consistent with and integral to the making of art—trimming excess to convey essential features and processes. It is an ongoing and pivotal discipline, a goal of the research, and a primary feature of its quality.

The distilling discipline is especially applicable to artistic inquiry, which potentially generates extensive material and content that must be culled for inclusion in the final presentation of the work. Enormous and meandering texts are also apt to reinforce bias against artistic inquiry as lacking rigor.

The selective concentration of the overall research is one of the most challenging processes in the creation of dissertations and theses, and in my experience the inability to do it results in significant drawbacks in relation to impact. Thus, the process is a continuous focus throughout this book.

Just as a painter, even with the most figurative style, *abstracts* the forms and qualities that suggest the resulting representations, the same applies to writers, composers, musicians, dancers, actors, filmmakers, and artists in various other media who pare down experience to fundamental forms, eliminating extraneous things. They strive to extract the marrow of an experience. This artistic approach to abstracting can permeate all artistic inquiry and presentation.

Proposals

In my experience supervising planned academic research, I have found the doctoral proposal process to be of great value. As I have mentioned, one of my primary objectives as an advisor and dissertation committee chair, in addition to supporting research excellence, is doing everything possible to help advisees successfully complete dissertations and receive their degrees within a reasonable time. The creation of a clear, concrete, and concise proposal describing the research rationale and objectives, question(s), and methods of inquiry generates the essential structure of the work to be done.

The proposal serves not only as a guide to the ensuing research but also as a contract between students and their doctoral committees. It requires considerable distilling of the research objectives and experimental processes, all of which concentrate, stabilize, and accelerate the process of inquiry. The proposal also informs applications submitted to an Institutional Review Board (IRB) charged with assuring ethical standards and the well-being of research participants prior to initiation of the research.

With my advisees, I encourage a terse statement describing the aims of the research and the need for it, together with an empirical description of how they hope to do it. Whereas others will often do extensive reviews of literature in proposals, I recommend a brief statement demonstrating a clear grasp of the core issues and context, significantly more succinct than described above in relation to a literature review, addressing the essential work done by others that significantly relates to the proposed research.

Detailed coverage of literature in the proposal will deter from the more essential articulation of how the research will be done.

This planning of the inquiry is, as I have mentioned, contrary to my personal history of naturally emergent artistic experimentation and the future art-based research I see happening in more organic and unplanned ways outside higher education. I consistently discover in all forms of artistic practice, in addition to writing, that the content and ideas emerge from the work in a process that can be likened to a conversation. Authors consistently describe how the process of writing enables them to "see," develop, and refine their thoughts, which as D. H. Lawrence said, often take shape "unwatched." And in my writing, the process is rarely outlined in advance. But from a practical perspective, formal academic research projects ideally have defined beginnings and end points as well as required procedural milestones along the way.

My role as an advisor is to apply experience with the process to help advisees successfully complete it, with doctoral committees working as teams to further objectives that we have helped create and approve. In designing a proposal, I strive to keep it focused on uncomplicated procedures that maximize freedom of artistic exploration and discovery together with a supportive structure. Regarding my earlier question as to whether planned academic research can accommodate natural artistic processes, I think it can.

There will be situations where proposals may not work "as planned" and in my experience this can be an opportunity to revise the direction of the research to address issues not anticipated in the original scheme.

In addition to revising plans and methods based on the emergence of unexpected conditions, proposals can formally anticipate these occurrences and affirm their place within the inquiry, simply stating that in the event of significant unplanned developments, the committee will discuss and approve adjustments and changes in the research protocols. In this respect, the planned research sets the stage for new issues emerging from its implementation. The unexpected dimensions of the artistic process need to be embraced as predictable and potentially productive features of artistic inquiry.[2]

As I will later discuss in relation to pre-dissertation pilot projects and other forms of open-ended artistic exploration of research directions, there are various ways that planned academic research can accommodate natural artistic experimentation.

Questions and methods

As recommended throughout this book, art-based research methods are created in response to questions. They do not follow preexisting steps and structures prescribed by a fixed research method, all of which contradict the nature of artistic expression. We do our best at the start to put aside all the various research standardizations and ponder how to explore the questions most effectively through art processes designed to address them. Since most of the research I have supervised explores artistic practice, often with specific media and situations such as therapy or education, the primary focus tends to be established as we begin to create the research structure.

In building upon the issues regarding questions and methods as described in the previous discussion of research proposals, I want to repeat and underscore how they generate the overall architecture, direction, and purpose of the research. And where all research in the realm of human experience ideally creates methods of inquiry in response to research questions, this is particularly significant with art-based research, where every conceivable project will be shaped by the one-of-a-kind nature of artistic expressions.

In a chapter called "Doing art-based research: An advising vignette" in Ross W. Prior's book *Using Art as Research* (McNiff, 2018a in Prior, 2018b), I create a hypothetical advising scenario where I attempt, based on my experience, to draw together core elements that may apply to the broad spectrum of research possibilities. The issues described in the chapter are explored throughout this book, all of which reiterate my reluctance to suggest "the way" to do art-based research because of the unpredictable possibilities inherent to creative expression which, as I keep saying, correspond to the nature of empirical art processes.[3]

In the invented advising scenario, I pose examples of possible research questions based upon my experience in helping others express themselves naturally through painting and drawing: *How does simple gesture drawing emerging from repeated movement influence expression? Does it further spontaneity? Natural and authentic expression?*

Repetition in this sense does not involve exact replication but rather a spontaneous and rhythmic process where the body's movement sustains expression, welcoming variation and change, all originating from the initiation of action and reactions to it.

These questions offer an example of how a multidimensional art-based research project can emerge from simple and compact queries. In my studios, I find that people throughout the world doubt their ability to express themselves effectively in all forms of artistic expression, largely due to mistaken notions of talent and negative experiences and judgments from the past. And skilled artists often need help and support in exploring alternatives to their habitual ways of working. I consistently discover, once again through natural experimentation, that elemental and sustained movement will reliably further authentic expression. I liken it to breath and other forces of nature. When the movement emanates naturally from the body, the mind tends to relax its grip on controls enabling a fluidity of expression.

Basic and elemental research questions can be explored in endless ways; thus, I do not want to suggest one model. I encourage my advisees to approach methodology as an integral element of their art, and as I have discussed, methods will extend from their art practice and questions.

We can also expand the possibilities of this example by modifying the questions to include movement-based repetition in art forms other than drawing and painting—dance, percussion, voice, performance, etc. Again, these examples are given to suggest the endlessly different ways questions can be explored and the vast possibilities for artistic methods of inquiry.

As discussed earlier, I believe that once research questions and issues are in place, the *why* of the inquiry, we then establish an empirical approach to exploring the *who*, *what*, *when*, and *where* of how they will be explored. Here is a selection of possible areas to be addressed in creating a description of research methods.

- Will the research be conducted by oneself, with others, or both?
- If there will be research partners, who will they be; how will they be selected, and will their identities be acknowledged; how will their rights and other research integrity issues be assured? In some cases, anonymity may be appropriate and with other

research partners it might be better to extend credit for their contributions.

- What art media will be used to explore the questions?
- How will the process of the sessions be recorded and documented, and who will do this?
- How many sessions and how long will they be, and where will they take place? How may the environment impact the inquiry?
- What type of artistic expressions will be generated? Will there be written transcriptions of verbal communications?
- Will the person(s) doing the research keep a journal throughout the process, and what kind?
- How will the person(s) doing the research organize, and reflect upon, and interpret the materials generated by the research?
- How might the art evidence be selected and presented in the dissertation?

In the following pages, I discuss a number of these method issues that characterize art-based research.

Presentation of the research and outcomes

As I have emphasized, the whole of an art-based research project is ideally conceived as an integral work of art. In the previous discussion, I described how I have navigated this issue within prescribed institutional formats. As a supporter of format and methodological freedom rather than fixed models of art-based research, I offer suggestions and principles that can span both standardized structures and the breadth of artistic presentations.

I have been asked if it is possible to present an art-based research dissertation or thesis project by showing the art alone—the dance, painting, music, screenplay, film, performance, creative writing, etc. Since documentary films are often expositive and offer comprehensive information and reflection upon the issues and content being explored, it can be argued that they can, in some situations, address these needs even more effectively than text. The same may apply to other art forms, and to video documentation of research processes and outcomes as I will describe here, but I feel that within the context of formal academic research, text reflecting upon the artistic experimentation as the primary process of the research, will generally further impact. And additionally, even the most experimental institutions have this requirement. The text helps to contextualize the research, guide readers, establish the place of the work within the larger communities of practice, and further communication.

However, regardless of the presence or absence of expository text, the primary feature and contribution of art-based research is art evidence speaking directly, convincingly, and not being translated into something other than itself. Experience in higher education reinforces the need to guard against diminishing this principle. Within dissertations and theses, expository text can be presented without compromising the fundamental art process, and the degree of its use will most likely depend upon the institutional context and its requirements together with the nature of the project. Ideally, and in keeping with the principles encouraged here, the inquiry can be presented as an integral artwork comprising text and other forms of art evidence rather than separating the art process from reflection on it.

I can envision art-based research projects dealing with ambiguity and encouraging projective responses to projects that are not as clearly defined as I recommend here. If I am reviewing work of this kind within a formal academic context, and while supporting artistic freedom, I would like to know something about the goals of the research, questions, methods, and outcomes as perceived by the person(s) conducting the inquiry, rather than speculate about these issues. But within the larger context of art, and as demonstrated here through discussion of natural art experiments and their importance, a more complete and unconstrained expressive freedom can be considered as one of its defining qualities.

Within higher education, I look forward to a future of wide-ranging and imaginative inquiries, that further creative tension in relation to accepted forms of presentation. Regarding art-based research within the context of dissertations and theses, the final presentation will hopefully have the freedom to present the work artfully and realize an integral relationship with the process of artistic inquiry.

In organizing the description of the research, discerning curation of the art evidence is recommended. Efficient communication of the work will increase its impact. Although appendices can often play an important role in art-based dissertations, I strongly encourage including only selections needed to supplant the art evidence presented in the text, rather than compiling the bulk of the art often generated.

The culmination of the research, in my opinion, involves articulation of outcomes, presented succinctly and with reference to the guiding questions and methods. This terse encapsulation of the entirety then informs the abstract and introduction to the dissertation, and the overall presentation of the project. The process of identifying outcomes permeates the whole research experience but is fully realized in the concluding interpretation of the whole.

The subsequent sections on artistic reflection and video offer art-based alternatives to conventional analytic methods for determining core outcomes.

Notes

1. "If I had more time, I would write a shorter letter," is apparently first attributed to Cicero (106–43 BCE) but also voiced by Blaise Pascal, John Locke, Henry David Thoreau, Mark Twain, and others. For reference, see p. 103.
2. Since doctoral research proposals involving other people are generally reviewed by an Institutional Review Board (IRB), as previously described, I encourage a clear statement of how other people will be involved and that adjustments to the research questions can be made as the study progresses. If revisions to the plan significantly change approved protocols, consultation with the Board may be advised in keeping with institutional policy. See p. 106.
3. Perhaps I need to reconsider my insistence that, unlike science, art-based research does not seek to affirm laws since there is a consistency to this principle together with my earlier ironic likening of the unpredictable nature of the creative process to a scientific law. See p. 107.

7

Innovations Shaped by Experimentation

Solo and reciprocal inquiry with others

One of the decisions to be made when conducting planned art-based research is whether the inquiry will be done by oneself or also involve others. All art-based research, by definition, involves the artistic participation of the person(s) doing the research as a primary form of inquiry.

The academic research that I have formally supervised has been done according to a proposal and plan created in advance. In most cases, the direction has emerged from more open-ended and spontaneous artistic practice and/or from previous experience in working with others. And in an institution where I supervised many dissertations, the final dissertation plan for art-based research has been tested and explored in advance by a solo pilot project. All of this work differs from my personal artistic experimentation, where there were no programmatic and formal requirements to be addressed and where virtually everything emerged unplanned in response to situational needs, suggestions, and inspirations.

As described earlier in relation to my informal artistic inquiries, significant research can take place on a solo basis. However, with doctoral research in various applied art disciplines such as therapy, education, and health care, which provide services to other people, there is a programmatic assumption that those undertaking the research will experiment with others. I have found that students, mine included, have approached the work in this way and have not considered the possibility of working exclusively by themselves, since their goals are largely concerned with perfecting professional practice with others.

As with my earlier description of research "not being about me," the person doing it, I had also assumed research in the realm of applied art disciplines would involve exploring and testing methods with other people. There are valuable social and peer-learning elements generated by collaboration with participants in a communal effort versus solitary work. But it can be asked whether veracity is dependent upon multiple participants? And can artistic inquiry, the majority of which has happened independently throughout history, sometimes be likened to an individual scientist working in a lab?

My personal experience, as described earlier, resulted in significant discoveries happening both when working by myself and creating with others (McNiff, 2003). But it is important to emphasize that formal research involving human relations and services generally occurs within academic and professional institutions, where, other than the fine arts, there is an expectation that protocols will involve other people.

However, as I mentioned, I have always encouraged my doctoral advisees to become involved in their own free artistic exploration as a discovery process in establishing a research direction. I was able to engage them in a pre-dissertation art-based research studio course where they did this with the support of a group of peers. The process was of major value in formulating research objectives that emerged naturally from their art, their experience, and future aspirations. The process confirmed what I earlier described as art's "function as articulator of the soul's uncensored purpose" (McNiff, 1992, pp. 4–5), not always in the forefront of present consciousness.

Solo artistic inquiry also played a consistent and vital role in the pilot projects my advisees were required to do as a qualifying procedure prior to developing a doctoral proposal. Where most students in the doctoral program, pursuing more conventional social science research, conducted their pilots with other people as they would with dissertations, the requirement offered an opportunity to perfect art-based methods before introducing them to others. The pilots were so successful and practically helpful that I encouraged my advisees doing art-based research in another program to include them as part of the qualifying papers that were required before developing a dissertation proposal.

The pilot project requirement, neither designed nor intended to be used as an individual art-based inquiry, became the most significant advance that I experienced in furthering planned doctoral research. I doubt that I would have conceived of this formative step without the mandatory structure and the resulting incentive to do something creative and useful with it.

In addition to aiding the identification of a research direction, the solo experimental work was of major importance in perfecting, fine-tuning, and adjusting methods to be used with other people. And as students have consistently affirmed—How can we ask people to do things we have not done ourselves? Not only did the pilots shape methods and help the persons conducting the research feel more comfortable and familiar with the processes, but I consistently felt that in relation to the whole of the research, they were of major import, arguably even more impactful, and possibly more completely focused on the empirical art processes. And perhaps most significantly, the solo pilots assured that the dissertations ensuing from them would be grounded in art-based research, defined as the use of artistic expression as a primary mode of inquiry by the person doing the research.

Experimentation with others offered comparative experiences and broadened the assessment of value, but it also added organizational, logistical, and formal procedural elements that did not concentrate as completely on the methods of inquiry. We also discovered that the solo pilots reliably generated the primary outcomes of the various studies. This result might be influenced by the more informal nature of solo processes, which correspond to the making of art. And contrary to the belief that the prior knowledge and familiarity of the person doing the research would bias the experimentation with others, we found that the pilots furthered more in-depth engagement together with insight in relation to the dynamics and outcomes.

Since the program requirement to do pilot studies set up the conditions for this discovery, the whole process can once again be likened to an unplanned natural art experiment. We had to deal with an external demand that unexpectedly generated one of the major research outcomes I have experienced in relation to art-based research. It is quite possible that another set of life conditions might evoke the same result, and perhaps others have, and will, come to similar conclusions through their experiences, since the process of artistic exploration transcends any one of us while including all. It is perhaps significant that the solo process, as I experienced it, has been tested by many different people, producing what I consider consistent outcomes.

In keeping with what I have emphasized throughout this text, I do not see the constructive results of the pilot project experiments as categorical and applicable to all forms of artistic inquiry. The process was influenced by my experience and artistic values, together with those of my doctoral advisees, and our common commitment to their different artistic inquiries in varied circumstances.

The previously mentioned innovations at the Melbourne Institute for Expressive and Creative Therapies (MIECAT) offer another closely related approach dealing with personal and exploratory artistic inquiry in contrast to more controlled and planned research procedures conducted with other people. The MIECAT community has created methods that blend individual and reciprocal artistic research with colleagues, a process described as "companioning" (Allen et al., 2021; Byrne & Fenner, 2023; Lett, 2016; McNiff, 2021b). The companioning partnerships involve working with one other person or small groups sometimes with two or three others. The experiential method is distinctly different than the conventional engagement of other people as "subjects."

In many ways, the co-creating process parallels what happens when a person works individually but adds the various dynamics of simultaneously making art with research colleagues and then responding to one another's creations. The resulting process corresponds closely with what I have always done in my group studios and when participants work with one or two others, and thus I resonate closely with it.

If the doctoral program where I advised students, which focused on individuals working alone in doing research with participants unconnected to the university, supported this form of collaboration between two or more doctoral candidates in the formal dissertation process, I would have encouraged reciprocal artistic inquiry as an option, since it is a natural extension of my studio practice and commitment to creating in community. This reciprocity, elements of which characterize art forms that require two or more people, can add significant dimensions to disciplines like creative writing and visual art, which generally involve working by oneself.

When experimenting with others in their art-based research, my doctoral advisees tended to cooperate with experienced colleagues, as with the MIECAT processes. They did not involve clients, which I felt would cause complications of dual relationships. The collegial nature of these relationships supported reciprocal creation and experimentation.

When involving others in research focused on methods of artistic practice to be used in professional work, I encourage engaging participants with some degree of knowledge pertaining to the issues being explored. The research in these situations is concerned with empirical ways of working, their impact, and how they can be perfected, and it benefited from the involvement of research partners with a certain degree of critical expertise. Thus, the doctoral research I supervised was thoroughly collaborative and, in many ways, like MIECAT's experiential companioning.

Since video documentation of artistic processes, often recorded by the person conducting research with others, has played a major role in the art-based research of my advisees, the videography can be viewed as a form of reciprocal and synchronous artistic expression. The process of recording and the subsequent editing are often approached as primary modes of artistic inquiry for the person conducting the research.

Both the MIECAT approach and my work are in sync with the growing emphasis on partnership and mutual relations in research dealing with human experience—"with" others rather than "on" them within a process of "co-operative inquiry" (Heron & Reason, 1997; Reason, 1999)—all of which can be viewed as an extension of experiential and adult learning traditions. Kurt Lewin was a major contributor to the development of a more wholistic emphasis on interactive participation and community inquiry (1946). The previously discussed "field" processes he explored correspond closely to life experience and arguably upend the more linear and hierarchical approaches of persons doing "controlled" research with "subjects," still prevalent in higher education.

The general emphasis on co-creation in research coincides with the discussion here about how individual persons create together with their environments, artistic materials, and other influences comprising an ecology of creation consistent with the idea that we never truly create alone as mentioned earlier. Considering the value and more complete inclusion of participating entities and forces can significantly expand our understanding of art-based research and its potential.

Artistic reflection in response to the research

Another major discovery emerging organically from my experience in advising art-based research is the use of artistic expression by the person conducting the research as a means of reflecting upon and interpreting the overall process. The subject of artistic inquiry has generally been approached by me and others with an emphasis on art as the principal exploratory process of the research, "a primary mode of inquiry," and not necessarily as a way of reflecting upon and furthering it. Although the engagement of artistic expression to interpret the research process, helping to manifest and identify significant results and outcomes, might be considered a "secondary mode of inquiry," I experience it as integral to the whole of the research from start to finish.

Artistic inquiry might then involve an interdependent and complete art process, including preliminary identification of a research direction as described here, the research experimentation, video documentation of sessions and editing of footage, reflection on the complete process, and the presentation of the research.

Based on my own ongoing process of discovery in relation to the practice of art-based research, I do not want to limit artmaking and future possibilities to a circumscribed scheme and propose yet another five fixed steps or phases. I present these aspects only as dimensions of artistic inquiry emerging from my ongoing experience and trust that future artistic experimentation will continuously take different forms. What is significant, in my view, is how the total research experience can take shape wholistically through art.

Artistic opportunities increase as we expand our thinking about the nature of research and its impact. Discussions about prescribed dissertation formats and research procedures can be enlarged to include conventions about how the ensuing research activity is interpreted. There is an assumption, even by some doing art-based research, that research texts (discussions, transcriptions, journals, notes) will be "analyzed" in keeping with the stock approach to "theme analyses" of "data" within social science research, as described earlier. The process can be done manually and with the use of coding technology, which introduces a scientizing and quantifying dimension.

With my advisees, I affirm the place of analysis in their research and our thinking about it, but not as an exclusive mode. We discuss the impact of technical procedures and their language, jargon, and embedded concepts about the nature of research, how they can bias the inquiry, and locate it within a paradigm that is not necessarily congruent with artistic expression. Analysis tends to involve breaking down experience to concepts, patterns, and other features. Responding to artistic expression is more than analysis. And the essential qualities of art are not restricted to themes which suggest underlying meanings, as contrasted to manifest and unique expression, which involves more than narrative structures.

We *experience* art and are often moved, inspired, and transformed by the unity of its expression. We respond viscerally with sensation, emotion, and imagination as well as with thoughts. The exclusive analytic reduction of an experience to conceptual themes is contrary to the nature of the artistic process. Together with the use of artistic inquiry as a primary mode of research and the focus on art itself as evidence, artistic interpretation of the whole experience distinguishes art-based research from standard social science frameworks.

Regarding the use of coding software, it might be utilized as one of many ways to respond to textual materials and can be helpful in highlighting patterns, identifying issues outside awareness, and so forth, but not necessarily as a standard, required, and primary mode of understanding. Repetitions of words and phrases can often be an extension of a person's habitual and sometimes redundant speech, while the superficial and mechanical counting process can be misleading. Therefore, I emphasize with my advisees that computer coding might be of use to them, but as a complementary contributor to the primary process of careful and sustained perceiving, reading, and responding within a living relationship with a text, art, and research process. Technical tools and artificial intelligence cannot replace the more essential reading and re-reading of a text where its overt and subtle features act upon our sensibilities in keeping with the formative and gestating processes of the creative consciousness.

In offering alternatives to exclusive theme analysis, I encourage interpreting, examining, studying, and responding creatively to the research experiences and the materials generated by it with all our faculties including imagination as well as analysis, contemplating the materials (transcriptions, video, artworks, notes, journals, memories) over an extended period of time—pondering how they address the research questions, act upon us, present new insights, and possibilities for practice.

The process of identifying and articulating the core features of the research is often challenging as I have emphasized, and it does not always lend itself to linear language and thought. The use of artistic intelligence as a way of dealing with the essential interpretation of the work emerged naturally and unscripted. It was common practice for my advisees to make personal art throughout the research process but artistic reflection on the core process of the research had not to my knowledge been considered, and it was not something that had been included in research proposals and plans.

Many students explored the making of art together with, or in response to, the artistic expressions of the people participating in their studies as a form of communication and affirmation during formal research sessions. Artistic responses were often a core element of their research methods and experimentation with others but not necessarily considered as a formal way of reflecting upon and interpretating the overall research project.

I was focused on encouraging students to think beyond the assumption that the research would be followed by the conventional data analysis and coding procedures described above. In contrast, I urged them to immerse themselves in reflecting upon the research process and the material generated, to live with it all as fully as possible, to read transcripts of conversations closely and repeatedly, since they would be involved in creating a text describing the process and outcomes.

The realization that artistic processes could be used to further this overall review of the process emerged incrementally, just as dreams enter to offer often abrupt alternatives to ingrained ways of thinking about experience. It ultimately converged into a natural and seamless extension of artistic inquiry that was of major import in furthering a more comprehensive understanding of the research process. Rather than shifting to "analyzing the data" of the artistic experimentation according to conventional social science procedures, as described above, the artistic inquiry was sustained into another dimension.

As with my formative and unplanned experiences of the 1970s as described earlier, the responses in various art forms (including creative writing, visual art, bodily enactment, sound and music, and especially video as described in the following section) furthered understanding and identification of results and outcomes in ways not possible through conventional analysis. It became a major feature of the art-based research I supervised and raises yet more possibilities for the future.

When the scheduled research sessions were completed, together with the documentation of them, it was natural for the person conducting the research to make art in an open-ended and spontaneous way without the pressure of any kind to generate results. The relaxation of controls and specific objectives not only served as a fluid transition to, and preparation for the next phases of the research but the making of art unexpectedly created a space and process for the "results," patterns, and discoveries of the research to cohere and manifest themselves. Reasoned reflection certainly has its place in interpreting the research process, but in my experience, it cooperates with all the other faculties operating in the various art forms responding to the work.

Just as I instinctively initiated artistic responses to reflect upon the work I was doing in art therapy practice and training—as a mode of inquiry and understanding as described earlier—others within the field have done the same, and the general practice has become increasingly mainstream (Allen, 1995; Fish, 2013, 2016; Moon, 1999; Nash, 2019). Therapists are becoming more consistently in sync with the substantive process of their discipline, themselves practicing what they strive to bring to others. Since the rationale for art in therapy is that it offers something different than discursive language and its narrative structures, it might be asked why these artistic modes of expression, reflection, communication, discovery, and understanding do not permeate all aspects of the discipline. Education and training in the various applied art disciplines have been grounded in personal artistic inquiry and experimentation, and now professional supervision, which has historically been a talking relationship, even in applied art practice, is now embracing artistic inquiry. Research is the next major and unrealized frontier.

Video and new media

I have emphasized throughout the previous sections how video and new media enable art-based research to realize its potential for documenting and studying artistic processes and presenting art evidence. As we discovered in the early 1970s (McNiff and Cook, 1975; McNiff, 1981b;), the opportunities presented by video, without exaggeration, can be likened to the impact of the microscope in biology and the telescope in astronomy. We worked then with video *Portapaks* producing black-and-white tape viewed through a monitor (TV screen) during "playback" sessions (Figures 7.1–7.3). The video technology was provided by Christopher Cook, director of the Addison Gallery of American Art, who like other performance and conceptual artists saw its potential to expand the role of art in life. He wanted to do the same in exploring its use in art therapy together with me (Newsome & Silver, 1977).

Where film had been used earlier in mental health to analyze behavior (Condon & Ogston, 1966), we used video to affirm it. Participants in our groups were able to see the process of their expression in movement, vocalization, performance, making visual art, and reading their creative writing. And some members of our group became involved in shooting the video, engaging it

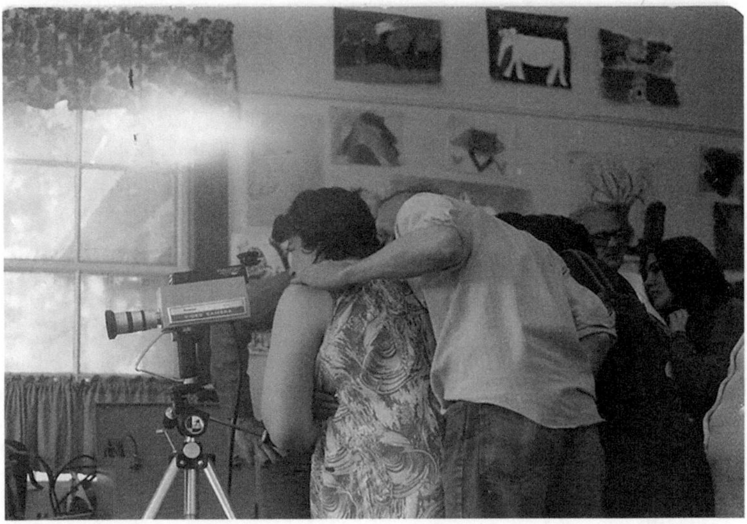

Figure 7.1: Danvers Art Cottage video session, ca. 1973. © Shaun McNiff.

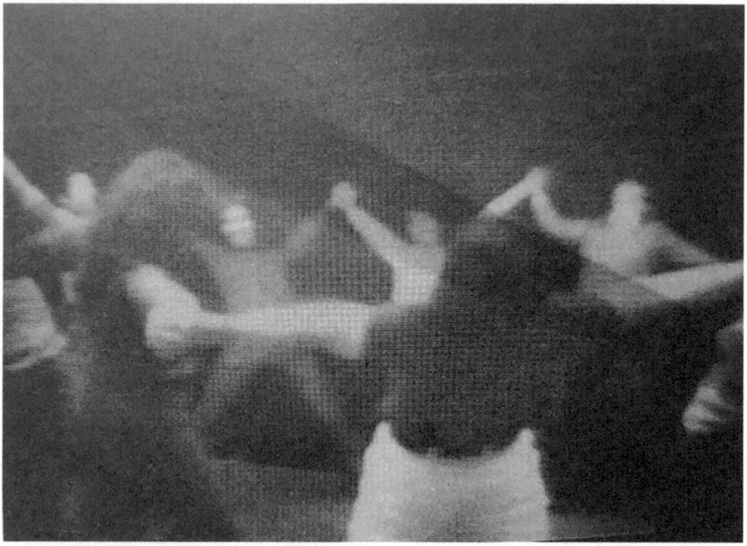

Figure 7.2: Addison Gallery of American Art movement experience on video monitor with an intentional blur effect, ca. 1975. © Shaun McNiff.

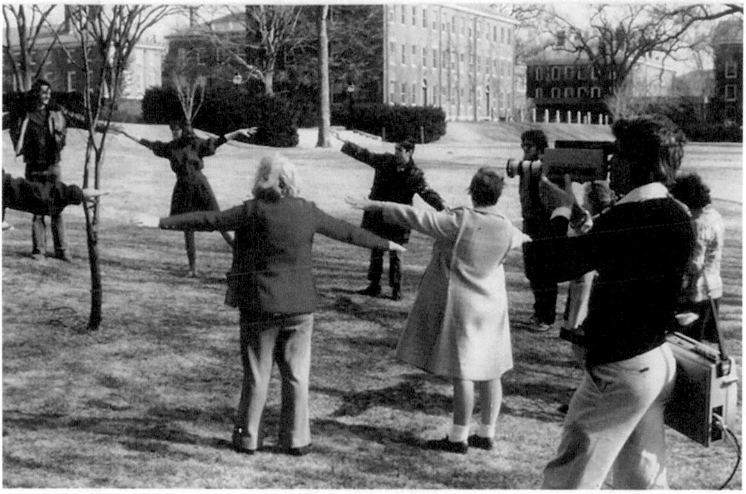

Figure 7.3: Movement outside the Addison Gallery with a portapak, ca. 1974. © Shaun McNiff.

as their primary art form. In-camera-editing and personal artistic interpretations were encouraged when staff and hospital artists recorded footage to be shown to the group at the conclusion of the artmaking when we gathered to view and reflect upon the video shown on a monitor. It became a playback ritual of community and artistic cohesion when the whole of the day's artmaking was consolidated into a collective work of art. The institutional support of the Gallery made the use of video possible, and this continued over the years in various settings with the capacity to provide access to the technology.

The more recent accessibility of compact and high-quality digital video, audio, and other new technologies, such as small, wearable action cameras recording from the perspective of the person making art—now expanding to inconspicuous video eyeglasses—have profoundly augmented the use of media in all forms of art-based research. The new media and their artistic uses are developing fast. The potential of video as a primary mode of art-based research is unlimited, and I do not want to interfere by suggesting preferences or models, in accordance with this book's encouragement of artistic inquiry corresponding to the limitless possibilities of artistic expression in any medium.

I will focus here on the use of video in conjunction with other art forms and explore the significance of being able to record artistic action, the role of the editing process in reflecting upon and interpreting artistic processes, and the enhanced showing of empirical art evidence in the presentation of the research. In this respect, I am suggesting that video and other new media can flip the paradigmatic assumption that the use of artistic expression in applied art disciplines must be explored through social science formats.

Confidentiality can be a primary concern in relation to video. In our earlier use within art therapy, only involving participants choosing to be involved, great care was given to consent, signed release forms, and various other legal protocols. Consideration was also given to where and how the video would be shown to others, and this again was based upon consent.

As I previously described in relation to the doctoral research I have supervised in recent years, we do not involve "human subjects," clients, or any other possible situations where the persons conducting the research may have dual roles and responsibilities. When working with others, the participants are viewed as research partners, and they are generally, as mentioned earlier, professional colleagues or others who can inform the experimental activity, as I have mentioned.

But where confidentiality may not be an issue when involving colleagues, I discovered from the very beginning of my work with video, and especially with the visual arts, that the relatively anonymous close-up showing of hands and bodies using art materials heightens and focuses the presentation. The same applied to playing musical instruments. The development of wearable cameras has greatly expanded these possibilities. My experience with video in doctoral research has shown that even when participants are willing to be identified in video and acknowledged for their contributions, there are many situations, which of course do not include those involving facial expressions, where there can be advantages to a certain degree of anonymity, which may further concentration on bodily gestures. These videography issues, together with others beyond our scope here, will influence how new media are used in the future to inform research questions and the methods exploring them.

The impact of video in documenting the making of visual art, generally perceived as a still medium, has been especially transformative in easing the bifurcation of process and product (McNiff, 2018c). Gaps between art forms are also narrowed with the visual arts now capable of joining movement, drama, music, and the reading of creative writing in showing the action of creation, not to mention the dance, enactment, sound, and poetic qualities of making physical art objects.

When first experimenting with video during the 1970s, I saw how it can be an integrative medium capable of holding many dimensions of the art process. It enables kinetic and temporal expressions to assume empirical permanence. And what have historically been viewed as "still" art objects can now be experienced from the perspective of action and progressive formation within specific moments and environments in time and place, and perhaps most importantly showing the presence of the artist.

Video recording adds yet another feature reinforcing my emphasis on how we are never truly alone when creating by ourselves. It allows solo activity to simultaneously involve different perspectives on the acts of creation. Cameras can be viewed as witnesses offering independent and animated views of the artistic action, as described earlier.

It is important to underscore how video recordings, like people and their perceptions of an experience, operate from vantage points and do not offer what might be considered objective accounts. The expansion of perspectives in the documentation of art process affirms how actions cannot be completely captured by any one observational stance or combination of several, all of which influence the structure of what is perceived. These conditions can be viewed as another research outcome, perhaps linking art to quantum reality, where the acts of observation influence what is perceived. Additionally, video and film will present what is recorded through the qualities of digital media viewed on a screen, which in turn affects the nature of the expression.

Despite technological advances of new media, the resources have been underutilized, especially in the visual arts, where research and publications continue to exclusively show still visual images together with text. Support for more complete exploration of the creative process in no way disregards research concerning visual art objects, as demonstrated by Arnheim and many others, including myself, whose relative permanence furthers their appeal and lasting power.

My doctoral advisees focusing on the visual arts have immersed themselves in the new technology using both wearable and mounted cameras, which document the making of paintings, drawings, and sculpture naturally and unobtrusively from multiple vantage points (Figures 7.4 and 7.5).

And when involving others in experimental sessions, the person conducting the art-based research often gets behind a camera and participates as another maker of art in documenting the process together with the stationary mounted cameras and participants wearing action cameras, or the new video eyeglasses, which I have not yet used. For many years, I have encouraged filming the process of painting to explore new dimensions of inquiry and understanding, and I have been taken aback by what my advisees have done with the most recent technology as self-taught video artists.

When asked how higher education can prepare students to do art-based research as distinguished from conventional social science instruction, I have considered training in video recording and editing. But independent exploration may have advantages in

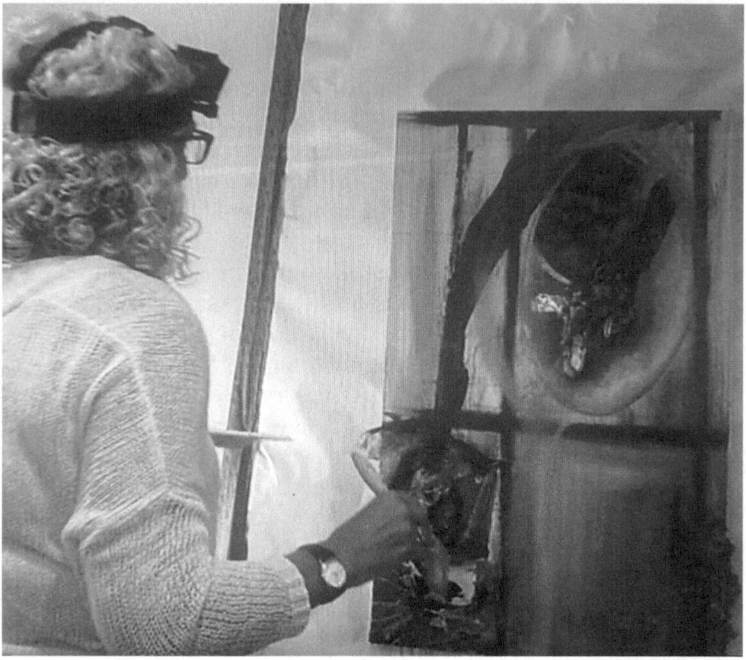

Figure 7.4: Video screenshot of Abby Miller painting while wearing a camera, 2020. Photo credit: Abby Miller.

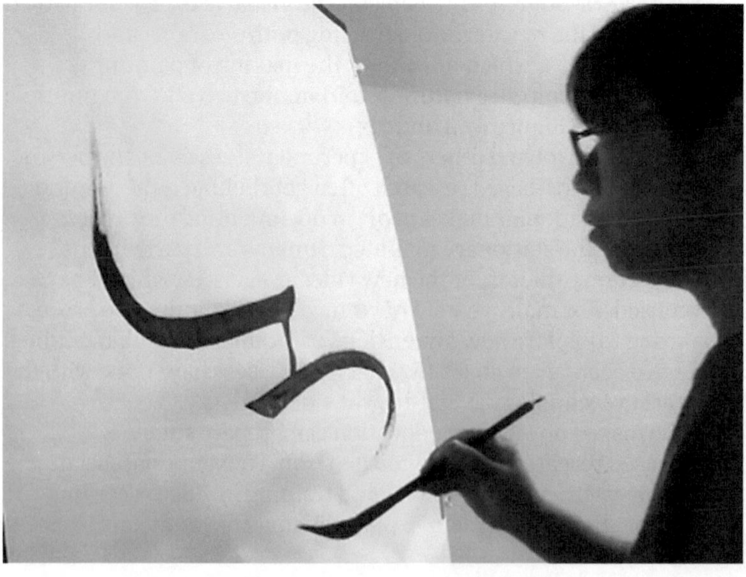

Figure 7.5: Video screenshot of Rumi Ito painting and being recorded by a stationary camera, 2021. Photo credit: Rumi Ito.

relation to originality with technological advancements enabling self-taught users to create high-quality art. In addition to documenting action, digital video, and especially wearable cameras, facilitate the instantaneous creation of still screenshots of a painting's evolution (Figures 7.6 and 7.7).[1] The plethora of images and video footage presents beneficial challenges in dealing with the material.

Editing and reflecting upon video footage have significantly advanced art-based research, offering important alternatives to conventional analytic methods of social science as I have described. Where in the past editing required training and access to complicated equipment, it can now be done with user-friendly and intuitive programs on small devices and computers. All these advances are furthering total accessibility.

I have encouraged my doctoral advisees to approach editing and reflecting on video footage like filmmakers working to achieve quality expression and impact. And regarding the process of reflecting on research sessions and outcomes, viewing and editing of video footage has become a primary and consistent way of artistically

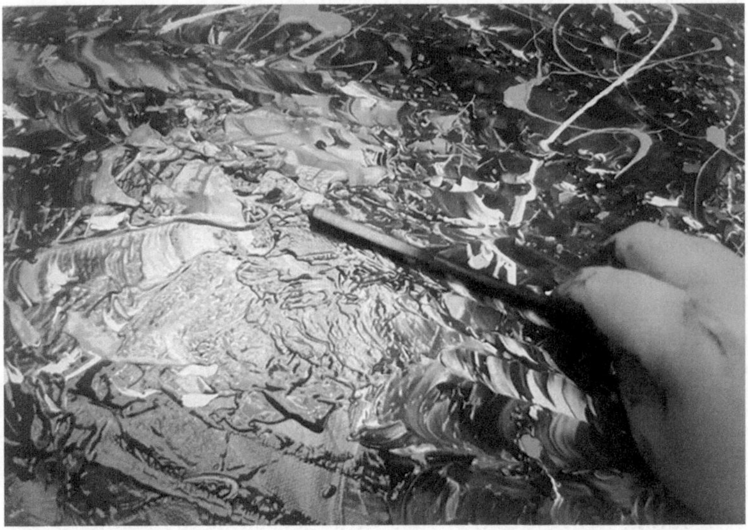

Figure 7.6: Video screenshot of Melissa Hedlund Nelson painting. Video taken from her wearable camera, 2020. Photo credit: Melissa Hedlund Nelson.

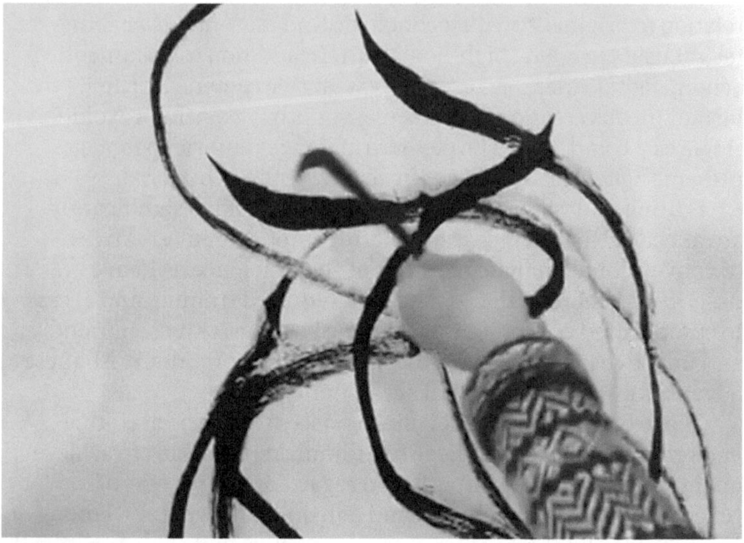

Figure 7.7: Video screenshot of Rumi Ito painting. Video taken from her wearable camera, 2021. Photo credit: Rumi Ito.

interpreting the overall research process as described earlier. In accordance with the sustained emphasis here on the significance of natural art experiments, the role of video editing as a primary mode of artistic interpretation and understanding of the research process emerged organically from the practical use of the medium—the recording, viewing, and editing of footage. It was not planned.

In contrast to the earlier discussion of the assumption that research will exclusively analyze "data," the editor-artist contributes a new expression fashioned from the various materials created in the experimental sessions and recordings of them. The edited video strives to artistically and concisely elucidate the essence of the processes being examined.

One of the many things that video recordings offer is the opportunity to look and relook over extended periods of time. I encourage living with the video without rushing to judgment. Sustained inquiry can help to confirm interpretations and expand them. It can also challenge reflections, offering revisions or alternatives.

Video complements the review of transcriptions of discussion and expands narrative accounts with the opportunity to reflect upon gestures, pauses, various physical expressions of emotion, together with subtle communications between people, objects, and surrounding environments, and various other nonlinear qualities. When working with extensive footage, I encourage the identification of seminal sequences or instances that I liken to Henri Cartier-Bresson's reference to "decisive moments" in photography. In this respect, the editing of video offers an artistic mode of interpretation, reflection, and presentation that aligns closely with art processes. The artistic process of creating an engaging video and clear presentation of decisive footage is apt to correspond to the identification of research discoveries and outcomes.

After recording sessions as described above, usually from multiple perspectives, my doctoral advisees study the footage by repeatedly viewing the whole over time, taking notes, creating instructive screenshots, identifying segments that address research questions, and possibly present unexpected issues and insights. In my experience the preliminary objective is to develop a sense of the overall research outcomes and identify footage that illuminates them.

The editing process usually begins with the creation of video presentations that roughly gather pivotal segments of video, and generally screenshots and pauses will be included for the purpose of focused viewing of footage. A defining quality of artistic inquiry is how the process of creating a compositional whole, in this case, editing video, furthers discovery, awareness, and identification of essential issues through the selection and integration of various contributing elements as I described in the preceding discussion of the artistic interpretation of the research process. Formative thinking and creation happen through the editing process: selecting the most relevant content and constructing the video to persuasively present evidence elucidating a thesis, all of which constitute artistic thinking and communication.

In generating these first edited video presentations, I encourage concision but with considerable flexibility in terms of viewing this phase of the work as exploratory. When involving others as participants in the research, these first edited tapes are created to be shared with them and reviewed together with the person/s conducting the study. The participants thus become primary research partners, helping to identify outcomes and how the work addresses research questions. When conducting the research by oneself, colleagues can be invited to participate in the review of the video.

One of my principal recommendations in relation to video editing and creation is complete emphasis on authenticity, *cinema verité*, and natural presentation of the visual and auditory recording. I stress with my students how, as a viewer, I am fascinated with this pure and essential focus and how distracting recorded music, text, and other supplements tend to be. The research is not about "entertaining" audiences, although I do find myself more artistically attracted to organic media. I accentuate how research partners and future audiences will be viewing the video because of their interest in the issues being explored. However, I do encourage sensitivity to attention spans and the need to distill, consolidate, and try to select illustrative segments to view with others. I do not recommend categorical limits in terms of video length. Relatively raw and unpolished compositions are fine when we make what might be described as the *first cut*. These preliminary videos tend to span 20–30 minutes.

In situations where the research is conducted in individual sessions with participants, there are generally reflective discussions taking place immediately after the meetings to discuss the experience without looking at the raw video, which would introduce many new features. With the research of my doctoral advisees involving other people as partners, the typical experimental sequence tends to involve four individual sessions with three or four participants. The reflections after a session reliably help to identify what participants felt at the time, and they further identification of essential features that will contribute to the subsequent viewing and editing of video. When preliminary drafts of the edited video documenting the whole sequence of sessions are completed, my advisees for the most part meet individually with participants to review the preliminary video.

If the research sessions involve groups, the members may meet after each session to reflect on their work together, again without viewing the unedited and often extensive video. The person conducting the research will then meet individually with each group member after the group experimental sessions have been completed to view and discuss the edited video, and if possible, review it again together with the whole group.

As I discovered with the earlier experimentation with video in therapy, viewing an edited presentation tends to affirm the contributions of participants while stimulating reflection, insight, and comment. And once again, I have found that compact and aesthetically stimulating video is more likely to generate creative and insightful reactions than long and more literal showings of sessions. Rather than exhaustive and unmediated coverage, I recommend editing that furthers the depth of engagement. Although some might consider this approach manipulative and perceive the editing of content as imposing a bias, the process relates back to earlier discussion of how—every vantage point entails a degree of non-objective selectivity, and the thoroughly personal artistic inquiry must also transcend the individual if it is to be useful. As artists, we create from our different places in the world, doing our best to generate quality expressions that connect with the needs of others.

Even when participants are unconditionally willing to give their time to view extensive footage, it may not be as productive as engaging a terse and carefully crafted distillation, which in some cases generates an interest in multiple viewing and replaying segments identified as particularly significant.

These various viewings and discussions are fundamental to identifying the final outcomes of the study and the video footage and screenshots illuminating them. The person conducting the research then creates what we call the culminating video, ideally five to ten minutes in length, to be included in the dissertation and public presentations. Minimal text is generally preferred—such as tersely stating research questions and outcomes—enabling the video to speak for itself as a complete exposition. While showing a sequence of action within a session or sessions may be helpful in certain instances, I support creating a composition that maximizes creative expression and a clear presentation of outcomes, which may diverge from chronological documentation of the action as it occurred. Various formats, such as multiple and simultaneous frames on a screen and altering the speed of action, may also influence impact.

A final draft of the culminating video might be shown with all participants being invited to meet to reflect on its efficacy and suggest possible adjustments. The ability to hold meetings of this kind, especially when distances are involved, is facilitated by digital platforms.

The various issues and procedures that I am describing here in relation to the use of video in the more general documentation of art-based research can become individual research projects, a richness of possibilities that I think affirms the revolutionary potential of the artistic use of the medium.

In developing the overall composition of a dissertation or thesis, video links are generally used in two ways: Firstly, as integral features of the text to illustrate points being made, and then as described above, to present a culminating video toward the end of the text when giving a summary of research outcomes together with concluding remarks about their implications. In my experience as a reader, the links to video within a text function like still illustrations (screenshots of action, visual art, photographs, passages from creative writing, and so forth) and are most effective when succinct footage supports a continuous and relatively uninterrupted reading of the whole manuscript. Longer video illustrations providing more detailed examples of a given situation may be included selectively in the appendices.

Just as our earlier experimentation with video in art therapy showed how skillful camera use and editing influence the expressiveness of the resulting video, the same applies to its use in research. Quality presentations will affect the influence of the art evidence.

Despite a reluctance to selectively reference the dissertations of my numerous advisees, all of which I consider making important contributions to art-based research, and my understanding of it, I realize that readers are interested in seeing how others have pursued artistic inquiry through video and filmmaking. In addition to offering an example of a culminating research video where the art evidence speaks for itself, Serena Duckrow Fonda's publicly accessible film *Conversations in Clay* (https://m.youtube.com/watch?v=PytIFZVvIig) offers an inspirational artistic consolidation of a study exploring co-creation in the ceramics studio of a maximum-security forensic psychiatric facility (Duckrow, 2017).

The film and dissertation artistically deal with confidentiality requirements by focusing completely on the hands of participants working with clay in the studio (Figures 7.8 and 7.9), reinforcing the previous mention of how the vantage point can enhance perception of artistic action even in situations where privacy is not a priority.

The impact of close-up frames of artistic action was affirmed by another of my dissertation advisees, Michal Lev who found that

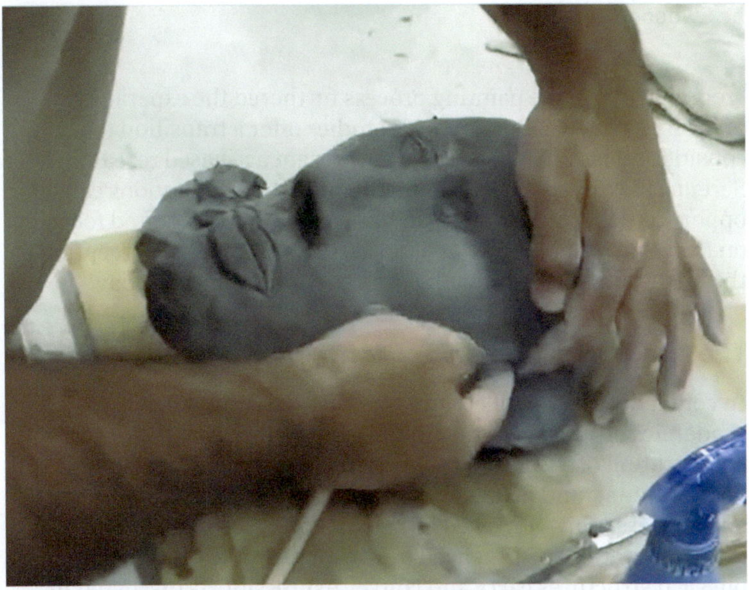

Figure 7.8: Video screenshot 1 showing a close-up view of a participant working with clay, 2017. Photo credit: Serena Duckrow.

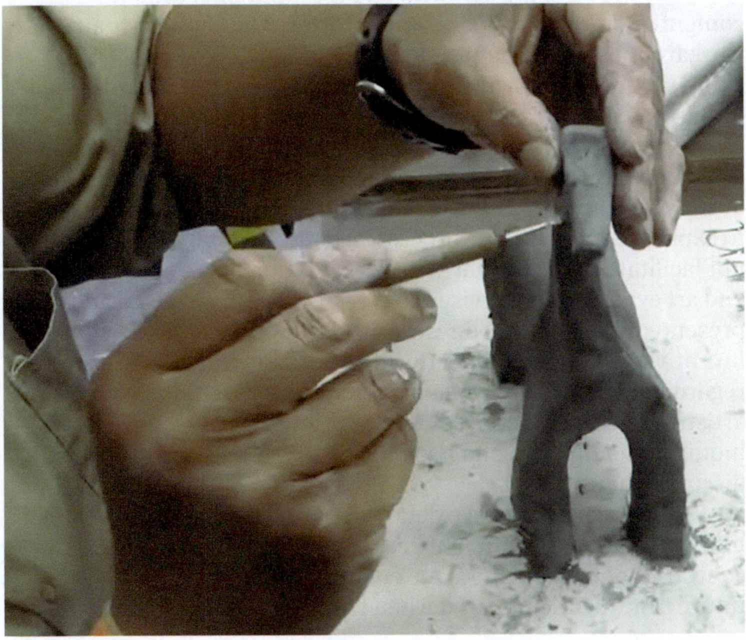

Figure 7.9: Video screenshot 2 showing a close-up view of a participant working with clay, 2017. Photo credit: Serena Duckrow.

"zooming in" on the painting process furthered the experience of intimacy (2019). Both of these studies offer a transition to considering how to most effectively present art-based research, with Serena Duckrow Fonda's film highlighting how limitations can offer opportunities for innovation, in this case with the required focusing on the relative anonymity of hand gestures deepening perception of the tactile, kinetic, and shaping process of creating with clay.

The integral relationship of form, content, and process

In concluding these reflections on practice within formal academic settings, I want to reinforce my emphasis on the *artistic* presentation of art-based research and the integral relationship of form, content, and process. Ideally and logically, artistic content and processes are conveyed by artistic form. And the impact of the presentation is influenced by the quality of form since the physical structures carry and convey expression as discussed in the preceding sections. Yet, as I have described throughout this book, academic and professional research in applied art disciplines generally requires the paradoxical presentation of artistic content and process in non-artistic forms. The challenges and workarounds can be daunting.

In my scholarship over the years, I have not been constrained in this way in contrast to my doctoral advisees who have been required to follow standard social science formats with the attendant language and concepts as described in this discussion of current academic practice. The structures do enable students to explore art and artistic processes, but the overall format does not facilitate an integral artistic presentation of the research and art evidence. My advisees have effectively conducted and presented their art-based research within the strictures, and their inventiveness has significantly influenced my thinking, especially regarding video and new media, artistic interpretation of the artistic experimentation, solo exploration, and personal artistic inquiry extending beyond itself to inform more general practice as discussed here.

Paradoxically, as I have detailed, the antithetical requirements have stimulated invention in keeping with my sense of how contraries define and motivate creation. However, we look to the future of academic research when these constraints no longer exist and where artistic inquiry in all academic settings is free to fully present the work artfully and directly.

Art is classically understood as involving skillful and imaginative creation in its various forms, all aspiring to realize quality expression. The issue of artistic quality, as I have said, also affects the degree to which the expressions impact audiences. And as I have shown, the quality principle similarly applies to the influence and value of art-based research.

An emphasis on the quality of artistic experimentation and presentation may, at first, seem to contradict my support for universal access to art-based research, which will be explored in the following section. But I believe the ability of an artistic inquiry to engage, inform, inspire, and influence audiences, what we might offer as an operational definition of quality that differs from the more conventional and exclusive emphasis on virtuosity, will prove to be consistent with support for accessibility.

Art is an imaginative process, realizing innate urges for expression, creation, and discovery, which are inseparable from the forms emerging from them. Some might say, in the interest of encouraging universal access to artistic expression, there is value in focusing exclusively on the former without potentially inhibiting attention given to formal features. However, art is generally known for its outcomes and forms—what is created. I feel that the more authenticity and variety we experience in relation to empirical art outcomes, all striving for the most effective communication and engagement of others, the more compelling the research will be.

Note

1. Readers can experience the whole context of research conducted by Rumi Ito, Melissa Hedlund Nelson, Abbe Miller, and the forthcoming description of the work of Serena Duckrow Fonda and Michal Lev through the links included in the references to their dissertations which demonstrate the suggestions for practice discussed in this section and reflect the use of video by all my advisees. While the five projects are primarily based in the visual arts, they give considerable attention to the body, movement, breath, enactment, and the comprehensive use of video to document and interpret the research. I do not want to convey partiality to specific areas of professional practice since artistic inquiry applies

to all of life and as emphasized throughout this book, I encourage each person or group doing art-based research to create their thoroughly individual approaches to inquiry rather than the common practice of following pre-existing methods—including what I have done with others. Additionally, most of my dissertation supervision over the past two decades has been within an institutional setting, that although supporting artistic inquiry, requires the IMRaD format. While my advisees have navigated the mandatory structure without diminishing the art base of their research, I again strongly encourage format freedom and complete integration of form, content, process, and presentation in future art-based research. For reference, see p. 127.

8
Looking to the Future

Who can do art-based research?

Does a person have to be a trained and/or "accomplished" artist to do art-based research? As someone whose career has involved supporting the artistic expression of many people throughout the world, experienced artists together with those with no previous involvement, I categorically say, no.

In my studio training groups, I repeatedly see participants just starting to explore artistic expression work effectively together with experienced artists. Those who are highly skilled in a particular medium will often become involved with unfamiliar art forms. Significant work is generated by everyone involved when there is commitment to the discipline and an emphasis on natural and authentic expression. In keeping with the Zen concept of *beginner's mind* (Suzuki, 1989), we invert assumptions about expertise, emphasizing how assumed experts have much to learn by experimenting in areas where they are less conversant.

In supporting engagement with unfamiliar art processes, I introduce organic and uncomplicated sources of expression that reliably generate quality work. The principal impediments that people tend to experience are self-doubt, feelings of vulnerability and fear in relation to the unknown, losing control, and so forth. In addition to emphasizing how we benefit from relaxing excessive control and doing our best to open to the unexpected, I encourage, as mentioned earlier, revisioning artistic expression as a force of nature and accessible as breath (McNiff, 2015). Perhaps most importantly, we support each other's expressions by affirming their distinctive qualities rather than judging them by various external and questionable standards. Within this perspective, unusual, unconventional, and raw creations are valued.

While supporting broad access to art-based research, I realize that most who are drawn to or considering this approach have generally established an art practice they feel offers productive possibilities for research. This has been the case with many of the graduate students I have supervised. They are committed to art and have life experiences confirming its intelligence and ability to further understanding for themselves and others.

I welcome broad participation and a multifaceted community of artists. Art will benefit from it. Just as I believe in universal access to artistic expression as a form of public health and education, where dedicated practice is a condition for realizing the benefits, the same applies to those without art experience who hope to become involved with art-based research.

In addition to encouraging the participation of artists without institutional training in all facets of artistic inquiry related to human understanding, I envision studies where they might have a certain firsthand "authority" (McNiff, 1993), such as exploring their own process of becoming involved with creative expression—How they got started? Challenges encountered? Setbacks and inhibitions? What worked and helped sustain involvement?—and so on, with a potentially vast array of possibilities to explore in relation to establishing an art practice.

I do my best to revision the expert stereotype when introducing students to art-based research. I say, all of us have areas of in-depth personal expertise, an "authority of experience" (McNiff, 1993) from having undergone particular life processes which no other person knows in exactly the same way.

Natural art experiments emerging through practice

I realized on completing an early draft of this book that the focus on natural art experiments, that I had considered writing separately as a concluding chapter, was present as an integral and primary feature from the start in descriptions of how my experience with art-based research has taken shape over the years, and in references to exemplary works by many others whose discoveries and innovations were developed from their art practice without necessarily being perceived as formal research. These descriptions of natural art experiments, "true to form," emerged unplanned and "naturally" through the process of writing, yet another example of how artistic expression gathers and transforms a complex of participating elements through a gestating creative process.

And as I have said, the creative tension between artistic processes and required academic procedures within the social science context significantly contributed to establishing what we now call art-based research, all of which can be viewed as a natural art experiment. Everything I have done to further art as research has been informed by the productive, defining, and motivating role of conflict—a process in the human sphere corresponding to the transformative function of disturbance in nature.

As I began to consider how to give an account of how natural art experiments are constantly happening in the world, I came upon two random examples in just one morning of reading the news: A Brooklyn painter, Rusty Zimmerman, doing 200 free portraits of neighbors to further a sense of community (Lastoe, 2024), a neighborhood art commitment we also see with Tyree Guyton's transformative Heidelberg Project in Detroit which has been sustained since 1986 (Whitfield, 2024); and an Iraqi composer and self-taught violinist, Ameen Mokdad, risking his life in 2014 Mosul by responding to the "need" to create, stating, "I cannot imagine any healthy life without art" (Shapiro et al., 2024). When his instruments were destroyed by those who occupied the city and banned music, Mokdad invented and built a new one with available materials.[1] Zimmerman and Mokdad clearly fulfill Neil Postman's previously mentioned research standard of having a story to tell, and Gadamer's definition of truth as a life-changing event supported in these instances by considerable art evidence.

Although these artistic initiatives may not have been undertaken as research projects, they exemplify what can be viewed as experiments constantly taking shape in life and enriching our experience of it. They suggest that the most important frontier for free and unfettered art-based research may exist in creative acts and projects happening naturally outside what is currently recognized as research. The two examples discovered by chance compare favorably to the total body of current academic and professional research in relation to art and well-being.

Within my community of colleagues, one of the most remarkable initiatives has been the ongoing work of Debra Kalmanowitz and Bobbie Lloyd over the past 30 years bringing art to areas of political conflict, social upheaval, and natural disaster throughout the world

(Kalmanowitz & Lloyd, 1997, 2004). They began in 1994 by creating "portable studios" in Bosnia, Croatia, Kosovo, and Slovenia in the former Yugoslavia and expanded to a global focus on making art in war-torn regions. The project emerged in response to turmoil and was shaped through practice and experimentation as described earlier in relation to the development of the graduate program I established in the 1970s. It was initiated to address a pressing need and not necessarily as research.

In the foreword to *Art Therapy and Political Violence*, I wrote: "The suffering of people living in crisis and their needs for expression and support conclusively show that a socially responsive vision of art therapy cannot be enclosed with a tidy container of [clinical] methods" (McNiff, 2004, p. xii). I realize now that the same can be said about research, where it is necessary to be closely connected to the unpredictable, uncontrollable, and dynamic events of lived experience and respond to them as effectively as possible.

In an account of how the portable studio concept and process emerged, Kalmanowitz and Lloyd described how they felt "humbled" and taken aback by the conditions people faced and were guided by their personal art experiences and what they had learned over the years in creating therapeutic studios for others.

They were "unclear" as to what they could "offer" (Kalmanowitz & Lloyd, 2004, p. 123) but "aware of carrying the spirit of a therapeutic studio as well as a responsibility for activating" the creative process in whatever context their sessions were offered and with available materials of expression (2004, p. 111).

They explicitly state how they needed *to create the studio environment together with the people they served*. The project emerged as a process involving all participants, illustrating that the artmaking of art-based research may involve collective creation and new ways of working with others. The documentation and study of a project of this nature is much more than what would be described as a case study. It entails a process of co-creation and experimentation with new ways of serving communities of people in crisis through artistic expression. Every participating person and event contribute to the art experiment, which takes shape naturally.

The work of Ruth Mateus-Berr in Vienna offers another exemplary team project. Among its many groundbreaking accomplishments it models how "artistic research," coordinating numerous participants working in various art forms can involve careful planning together with responding to needs and opportunities emerging from practice—integrating "plan and chance" (Mateus-Berr, 2023, p. 344).

Mateus-Berr established DEMEDARTS (*Dementia.Empathy. Education.Arts.*) at the University of Applied Arts Vienna with support from the Austrian Science Fund. The project is committed to furthering social empathy for people living with dementia and improving their life experience (Mateus-Berr & Gruber, 2021).

The research offers artistic "portrayals" and "interpretations" of the dementia experience with the goal of both learning about the condition and changing perceptions of it (Mateus-Berr, 2021, p. 103). Among the Vienna group's many achievements are presentations of the research in various art venues, including the Venice Biennale, and the artistic use of digital media. The 2024 project catalog published on the internet sets a new standard for high-quality and accessible artistic presentation of research and art evidence (Mateus-Berr et al., 2025).

The sustained public and educational focus of the Vienna project are exceptional and a model for the future. The research exemplifies the idea of total artwork, *Gesamtkunstwerk*, and its use of many art forms in cooperation with a broad spectrum of disciplines, including education, social services, architecture, and medicine in personal and public settings, where all the participating processes are naturally entwined. The experimentation involves a complex of creation that is given the freedom to evolve organically in response to the changing social context.

One of many reasons I prefer the term "art"-based research is that the art process includes transdisciplinary artworks of this kind and boundless artistic possibilities rather than thinking only in accordance with established institutional forms—"the arts." I say this with great respect for dance, music, literature, visual art, and theatre, their traditions, and their continuing importance in the world and for me personally, but these entities as currently conceived do not necessarily present themselves as including the breadth of art and the interdependence of its many forms, each one in many ways containing and intertwined with the others.

Fortuitously, I was closely connected to the formative conceptual art movement in Greater Boston in the early 1970s. It expanded art processes to the whole of life, to ideas and artistic actions beyond the limits of conventional disciplines, all of which influenced foundational concepts for art-based research. The artists, including Don Burgy and Doug Huebler, embraced new media and a critical discourse as to the nature and purpose of art.[2] They informed my efforts to establish graduate training and professional disciplines based upon the integral relationship of all forms of artistic expression, as contrasted to the pervasive separation and departmentalization existing then and now.

When I met Christopher Cook in 1972, whom I have described as responsible for exhibiting the art of Danvers State Hospital patients at the Addison Gallery of American Art, he had just completed a year-long project directing Boston's Institute of Contemporary Art as an *artwork*, documenting the process with video, photographs, and various installations in a culminating exhibition. It was a major form of art-based research or artistic research, happening in advance of the terms being established, which serendipitously coincided with my early work.

When Cook returned to the Addison Gallery, he *adopted* the Danvers art therapy program in keeping with his vision of broadening the role of art in society. The experimentation at Danvers, as described earlier, was later expanded to a nationally recognized museum-based video art therapy program run in partnership with several mental health and youth programs in urban communities near the gallery engaging people he described as "neglected by society, not just by museums" (Figure 8.1). He referred to the project as research generating extensive evidence that "art has a 'fundamental integrating capacity' to help people function better" and that "the primary significance of a museum should be to help art get into the mainstream of life" (Newsome & Silver, 1977, p. 175).

We also collaborated with John Hagerty who, as a Harvard College student founded the Massachusetts Prison Art Project working with incarcerated men and women. Like our experimentation at Danvers State Hospital and the Addison Gallery, the prison project's staff, volunteers, and participants were immersed as co-creators of the total undertaking and demonstrated efficacy and changed social perceptions through the public exhibition of art evidence.

And in more recent years, I have had the opportunity to cooperate with Guo Haiping of the Nanjing Outsider Art Studio in

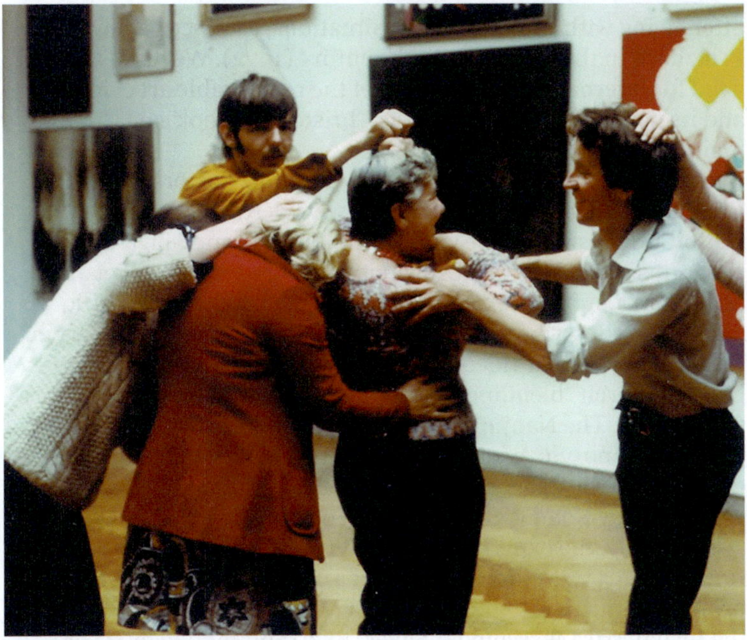

Figure 8.1: Addison Gallery group, ca. 1977. © Shaun McNiff.

Nanjing, China and Yamashita Masato of the Atelier Yamanami in Shiga-ken, Japan. The studio programs address the need to transform public perception of disability and mental illness in their respective societies.

I first became involved with the Nanjing studio when editing a journal edition on Outsider Art in China featuring the program. In addition to an interview with Guo Haiping, which includes works of art (Shushan, 2018), I conversed with Daniel Wojcik, professor of English and Folklore Studies at the University of Oregon, about "'grassroots' artistic expression and its redemptive power" (McNiff & Wojcik, 2018). We explored his book *Outsider Art: Visionary Worlds and Trauma* (2016) and the relationship of the Nanjing project to what has been called "outsider art" (also known as raw art, art brut, all taking place outside formal art institutions and, in my view, created by people truly *inside* the art process). There is a global presence of this work involving untrained artists often living with challenging life situations, as described by Hans Prinzhorn in the early twentieth century (1972). We discussed the need for international awareness of the remarkable art evidence and its potential to contribute, as Christopher Cook said, "to the mainstream of life."

One year later I was contacted by Harvard doctoral students, Raphael Koenig and Benny Shaffer, who were organizing an exhibition presenting the work of the Nanjing and Shiga-ken programs at the Harvard University Asia Center (McNiff et al., 2019).[3] In a publication accompanying the exhibition, Koenig and Shaffer described how they documented the making of art in the workshops with video and refer to the process as "practice-based research" blending "academic research and artistic practice" (2019, p. 8). The Nanjing studio, established in 2006, and Atelier Yamanami in 1986, exemplify how natural art experiments develop and then generate more formal academic *research* as conducted by Koenig, Shaffer, and Wojcik.

Similarly, the experimentation at the Addison Gallery of American Art was studied as part of a comprehensive research project conducted by the Council on Museums and Education in the Visual Arts (Newsome & Silver, 1977) and funded by several federal and private foundations.[4]

These experimental art projects tend to start with a sense of possibility in response to needs. They are complex living entities that are incrementally created within their particular environments involving many people. When I initiated the first graduate program to integrate all forms of artistic expression in therapy, education, and community service, we similarly began with a vision and sense of social need. In teaching courses as an adjunct faculty member in special education, students affirmed the value of art in helping children with various learning needs.

I view the graduate students in these first courses and those who enrolled in the program soon after, as co-creators of the emergent structures that grew exponentially in the ensuing years. Nothing would have happened without them and their affirmation and expansion of the needs to be addressed. Together with faculty, they created a complex whole that soon grew exponentially into much more than I could have imagined at the start. This experience perhaps highlights the interplay between planning and unpredictable emergence in artistic discovery, with the latter clearly being the primary creative force and outcome.

These collective creations demonstrate how the art process operates as an ecosystem, what Thomas Berry in calling for a new depth psychology of nature and creation, described as a "communion of subjects" (Berry, 1999, p. 82) "rather than a simple subject-object relationship" (Berry, 2006, p. 54). Consequently, in considering acts of creation in art-based research, it is important to expand the idea of artistic inquiry to a more comprehensive participation in an organic process of creation involving all forms of life, large and small.

These illustrations of experimental projects involving teams of people co-creating in every aspect of the work are offered to demonstrate how art-based research cannot be restricted to institutional assumptions about what constitutes the making of art. Since *research* and *evidence* have become so dominant in making decisions about social, educational, and health services, it is necessary to revise how the benefits of art can be best explored, defined, and demonstrated. In addition to academic art-based research which I support, we cannot be bound exclusively to it. I anticipate a more inclusive future open to the breadth of experimentation I hope to suggest here. We have not begun to realize the possibilities of the countless initiatives happening naturally—and often undocumented—every day throughout the world, demonstrating what art can do in challenging situations.

As I keep emphasizing, the art process tends to operate in advance of the reflecting mind, and we generally do not see the complete nature and significance of new and original efforts while immersed in them. Just as my earlier forms of artistic inquiry, and those of many other colleagues, were not necessarily perceived as research, the same applies to what I view as the frontiers of art-based research, inside and outside organized programs, where people respond artistically to needs manifesting themselves in the world.

All of the aforementioned experimental initiatives emerged organically and often intuitively in response to needs that could be addressed through art. They certainly did not follow the pre-existing procedures that generally characterize formal and institutionally recognized research today. And the people doing the work consistently create artistic vehicles for presenting it in the most socially impactful ways, with the outcomes invariably determined by the quality and relevance of the communications.

My recommendation for the future of art-based research is attentiveness to the process of creation in us and our environments, the persistent currents together with the random appearances and opportunities which often generate significant opportunities for inquiry and understanding. While supporting planned academic research and its many contributions, a complementary sensitivity to natural art experiments will further greater awareness of what is happening in life constantly.

The opportunities are vast as affirmed by Muriel Rukeyser who described how it can be "hard to hold for a moment the giant clusters of events and meaning that every day appear" (1996, p. 7).

Rather than being overwhelmed with the possibilities, we might consider responding with wonder and appreciation for the wealth of prospects and allow our engagement with the art process to lead, structure, and help us realize the purpose we may not yet fully realize. I wrote the book *Trust the Process: An Artist's Guide to Letting Go* (1998b) because I consistently witnessed how the artistic intelligence finds its way through what might be a challenging crucible of creation to our most authentic expressions and decisive acts. These emergent processes in us and others tend to happen naturally, often unpredictably. We must keep a prominent place for them in all aspects of art-based research.

"No rules" and the art-science relationship revisited

An unforeseen outcome of the process of writing this book has been a focus on the issue of "rules" in relation to research. In the social realm, rules matter. They are fundamental to civilization and behavior in all aspects of life including morality, the law, and sport. And in my teaching, especially when participants take risks with their creative expression, consensually validated rules assure support and sensitive responses. In a studio session, a student described how the rules were pronounced but she "never felt so free."

But do rules, and their constraints, apply to creation itself, imagination, and invention? Helen Frankenthaler, as mentioned earlier, insists on "no rules" in relation to art. Ursula Le Guin concurs—with the caveat that if a rule is helpful for those who feel they need direction, they can work with it, but in relation to solitary creation, apart from certain forms of music, she believes artists are free to set the rules guiding their creations (1989). Frankenthaler and Le Guin echo the Daoist tradition, which encourages naturalness and spontaneity in our interactions with the world as primary virtues. I think we can comfortably apply this ancient wisdom to the sphere of art and research.

The prescribed procedures that I describe as permeating current social science may be considered contrary to natural science. W. I. B. Beveridge in his classic *The Art of Scientific Investigation* maintains that scientific research is "an art." The noted Cambridge University scientist, while underscoring experimental rigor, supports the "no rules" position in describing how the transformative scientist tends to be pragmatic and imaginative and not one who "merely follows rules of logic and experiment" (1957, p. 102), which are unlikely to further discovery and innovation.

> Research is one of those highly complex and subtle activities that usually remain quite unformulated in the minds of those who practice them. This is probably why most scientists think it is not possible to give any formal instruction in how to do research … methods vary from one person to another.
>
> (Beveridge, 1957, pp. x–xi)

Beveridge, who significantly informed my early writing about artistic inquiry (1986a), reinforces how my formative thinking on research occurred in a time that was not pervaded by the current fixities of social science research. He is saying that the methodological uniqueness that I present as a defining feature of art-based research also characterizes scientific research. I believe he would share the position that the expansive academic industry of required instruction in approved social science research methods, bolstered by professional associations and accreditors, contradicts freedom of inquiry. As emphasized here, artists carefully study what others have done throughout history and while often influenced and inspired, they create their distinctive ways of working. I feel Beveridge would say that scientists do the same.

I surmise that he and Richard Feynman, who while as previously discussed, described natural science as involving imagination within tight-fitting experimental structures, would affirm Rudolf Arnheim's brief 1998 note to me, which encourages "keeping the concepts of art and science free from the usual restrictive definitions."

By necessity, rules tend to be categorical and can be distinguished from guiding principles, lessons learned, and wisdom transmitted from experience, which both art and science affirm. These bonds are important and highlight how the problems and tensions currently experienced in relation to art-based research in academic and professional institutions concern social science, not physical and life sciences.

The principle of methodological uniqueness emerged from the writing of this book as I considered what most clearly distinguishes art-based research from current social science practice. Perhaps, this book may inadvertently be of use to the latter domain, and particularly psychology, in establishing more realistic and inclusive research principles, and as I suggested earlier being more welcoming and aware of its artistic foundations.

Rudolf Arnheim articulated the methodological problems I address here in relation to his academic experience. In an essay called, "But is it science?" in his 1992 book, *To the Rescue of Art*, he reinforces my description of the relatively new institutional requirements for psychological research: "What one might call the Hippocratic Oath of the social sciences had fairly recently taken the form of a prescribed procedure ... extracting elements from their more complex setting and submitting their purity to an analysis" that fits "the rules of their scientific game" (Arnheim, 1992, pp. 175–176).

Clearly, his research establishing and advancing the psychology of art did not fit the scientific *zeitgeist* of the current era, or as Wittgenstein said, "game." In contrast, he wrote:

> Without remorse I have settled for the most careful observation and description of which I was capable, this being my definition of science. The ostensive method, the pointing with the index finger, the "Don't you see that ...?" is not without risk, but, particularly in teaching, it has always been my choice.
>
> (Arnheim, 1992, p. 181)

And in the spirit of this statement, I encourage focusing artistic inquiry on the direct perception of art evidence and responding to it as best we can.

In reflecting upon the relationship between art and science and their many shared features, I do not want to obscure their differences, which may in part involve the role of personal inquiry as discussed here. Affirmation of differences also affirms the integrity and existence of disciplines and guards against explaining and justifying one by another. Where both science and art can involve unique modes of inquiry and even personal experience, art-based research sustains and presents these features in their outcomes, while science generally strives to identify laws in relation to natural phenomena together with generalizable principles. Art is inherently varied, and science values replicability.

While recognizing the different approaches to artistic and scientific processes regarding goals, traditions, and operational processes, I am reluctant to support an inflexible definition of either domain. Although the disciplines may have fundamental differences, they are characterized by shared qualities as described here. To this day, the attempts at definitional differences have generally been misleading, superficial, and simplistically dualistic.

The stereotypic and exclusive distinctions persist. They include: art is subjective, emotional, and concerned with beauty and passion, whereas science is objective, factual, rational, dispassionate, and committed to generating new knowledge with methods informed by the laws of nature. In contrast, I have tried to show how both science and art share essential qualities, while also maintaining their complementary disciplines within the larger interdependence of the creative process and nature.

Ultimately, I believe it is important to maintain fluidity regarding definition. If science is open to its artistic and imaginative qualities, perhaps social science can do the same and support the full spectrum of human understanding. It can be said that both art and science elude categorical definition, and it may be advised, as I said earlier about art, to realize they can be best understood by avoiding the entanglements of explanation and concentrating on what they *do* and contribute to life.

In closing

If I step aside for a moment from the purpose of this book in making a case for the place of art-based research within academic and professional settings and do my best to open to the reality of experience and nature, it becomes clear that creation does not privilege one human mode of understanding, including art, over others. Exclusion and conceptual hegemony compromise the vitality of a collective creation much larger than any one of its contributors. As I emphasize throughout this book, we need them all to realize the fullness of intelligence and knowledge.

In 1804, Jean Paul Richter described genius as "all faculties ... in bloom at once" with imagination being the "faculty of faculties" coordinating the creative action (1973, p. 35). The creative scientists mentioned here seem to agree and affirm that if the different faculties are to realize their full capacity one cannot be subject to another.

In making the case for artistic inquiry within the research discourse, it is envisioned here as a participant in a greater whole where it continues a rich legacy of making contributions to understanding human experience and appreciating its place in the natural world. Rather than suggesting that art is superior in any way to other modes of inquiry, the recommendation of this book is to simply recognize that it may often contribute to other disciplines and be best suited to address certain questions, problems, and issues, and especially those concerning artistic practice and its ability to further human well-being.

Notes

1. Ameen Mokdad has been given a full scholarship for graduate study at Wesleyan University's World Music Program. See p. 139.
2. Since conceptual art flourished in using new technologies and materials not associated with usual art practice, I foresee artists, as mentioned earlier, using artificial intelligence tools in imaginative and provocative ways, exploring their positive and potentially negative dimensions and inventing ways to apply the technology to the expansion of art and its integral relationship to life. This is yet another front for future art-based research. Artistic intelligence (perhaps a complementary AI) and free experimentation may be perfectly suited to assuring the life-enhancing use of artificial intelligence to further human imagination. See. p. 142.
3. The articles cited regarding the Nanjing and Shiga-ken studios and published in the open access journal *Creative Arts in Education and Therapy: Eastern and Western Perspectives*,

present numerous illustrations of art which can be viewed through links to the publication. https://caet.inspirees.com/caetojsjournals/index.php/caet/article/view/96; https://caet.inspirees.com/caetojsjournals/index.php/caet/article/view/169/187. See p. 144.

4. The National Endowment for the Arts and the National Endowment for the Humanities in Washington, DC and in the private sector, the Rockefeller Brothers Fund, the Edward John Noble Foundation, and the Ford Foundation. See p. 144.

References

Albers, J. (1971). *Interaction of color*. Yale University Press.

Allen, P. (1992). Artist-in residence: An alternative to "clinification" for art therapists. *Art Therapy*, *9*(1), 22–29.

Allen, P. (1995). *Art is a way of knowing: A guide to self-knowledge and spiritual fulfillment through creativity*. Shambhala Publications.

Allen, J., Morrish, A., & Rumbold, J. (2021). Companioning the work: Living the legacy of Dr Warren Lett. *Journal of Applied Arts & Health*, *12*(1), 25–43. https://doi.org/10.1386/jaah_00055_1

Angelopulo, G., McNiff, S., & Prior, R. W. (in press). Art-based research: A conversation with Shaun McNiff and Ross Prior. In G. Angelopulo & L. Barkhuizen (Eds.), *Creative and expressive arts in therapy, education, professional practice, community and African culture*. UNISA/University of South Africa Press.

Arnheim, R. (1957). *Film as art*. University of California Press.

Arnheim, R. (1971). *Entropy and art: An essay on order and disorder*. University of California Press.

Arnheim, R. (1972). *Toward a psychology of art: Collected essays*. University of California Press.

Arnheim, R. (1974). *Art and visual perception: A psychology of the creative eye* (Rev. ed.). University of California Press (Original work published 1954).

Arnheim, R. (1992). *To the rescue of art: Twenty-six essays*. University of California Press.

Arnheim, R. (1998), letter to Shaun McNiff, July 31.

Arnheim, R., & Grundmann, U. (2025, February 24). The intelligence of vision: An interview with Rudolf Arnheim: The development of perceptual terms. *Cabinet*. https://www.cabinetmagazine.org/issues/2/grundmann_arnheim.php

Arts Council England (2026, April 11). A prospectus for arts & health. Arts Council England. https://www.artsandhealth.ie/policies-strategies/a-prospectus-for-arts-health-arts-council-england-pdf/

Atkins, S. (2012). Where are the five chapters?: Challenges and opportunities in mentoring students with art-based dissertations. *Journal of Applied Arts & Health*, *3*(1), 59–66.

Baars, B. J. (2003). The double life of B. F. Skinner: Inner conflict, dissociation, and the scientific taboo against consciousness. *Journal of Consciousness Studies*, *10*(1), 5–25.

Barone, T., & Eisner, E. (1997). Arts-based educational research. In R. M. Jaeger (Ed.), *Methods for research in education* (2nd ed., pp. 73–99). American Educational Research Association.

Barone, T., & Eisner, E. (2006). Arts-based educational research. In J. L. Green, G. Camilli, & P. B. Elmore (Eds.), *Handbook of complementary methods in education research* (pp. 95–109). Lawrence Erlbaum Associates.

Barone, T., & Eisner, E. (2012). *Arts based research*. Sage.

Barry, S. (2005). *A long long way*. Penguin Books.

Bast, G. (2020). Teaching artistic research for understanding and shaping society. In R. Mateus-Berr & R. Jochum (Eds.), *Teaching artistic research* (p. 9). De Gruyter.

Berry, T. (1999). *The great work: Our way into the future*. Three Rivers Press.

Berry, T. (2006). *Evening thoughts: Reflecting on earth as sacred community* (M. E. Tucker, Ed.). Sierra Club and University of California Press.

Berry, T. (2015). *The dream of the earth*. Counterpoint.

Beveridge, W. I. B. (1957). *The art of scientific investigation* (2nd ed.). Norton.

Bogard, T., & Bryer, J. R. (Eds.). (1994). *Selected letters of Eugene O'Neill*. Limelight Editions.

Borgdorff, H. (2012). *The conflict of the faculties: Perspectives on artistic research and academia*. Leiden University Press.

Brownell, A., Brownell, D., & Holloway Mulder, G. (Eds.). (2024). *Singing the psyche: Uniting thought and feeling through the voice*. Charles C Thomas.

Brownell, I., & Wilcoxen, W. (Directors). (1998). *A time to dance: The life and work of Norma Canner* [Motion picture]. Bushy Theater Inc.

Browning, R. (2024, January 31). *Andrea del Sarto*. Poetry Foundation. https://www.poetryfoundation.org/poems/43745/andrea-del-sarto

Burns, K. (Director). (2019). *Country music: A film by Ken Burns* [Film]. PBS.

Byrne, L., & Fenner, P. (2023). Emanation in creative practice: The impact of McNiff's construct of witnessing in an Australian setting. *Journal of Applied Arts & Health, 14*(3), 325–341. https://doi.org/10.1386/jaah_00145_1

Cassirer, E. (1975). *The philosophy of symbolic forms* (Vols. 1, 2, and 3). Yale University Press.

Cobb, C. (1984). *Cooperative creativity in the therapeutic relationship* [Master's thesis, Lesley College Graduate School].

Cobb, E. (1993). *The ecology of imagination in childhood*. Spring Publication. Columbia University Press Publications (Original work published 1977, Columbia University Press).

Condon, W. S., & Ogston, W. D. (1966). Sound and film analysis of normal and pathological behavior patterns. *Journal of Nervous and Mental Disorders*, *143*(4), 338–347.

Davis, M. (2024, March 5). *Miles Davis quotes: The jazz icon in his own words* [Video]. https://www.udiscovermusic.com/stories/miles-davis-in-his-own-words/

Duckrow, S. (2017). *Filmmaking as artistic inquiry: An examination of ceramic art therapy in a maximum-security forensic psychiatric facility* [Doctoral dissertation, Lesley University]. https://digitalcommons.lesley.edu/expressive_dissertations/30

Eisner, E. (1981). On the differences between scientific and artistic approaches to qualitative research. *Educational Researcher*, *10*(4), 5–9.

Eisner, E. (1997). The promise and perils of alternative forms of data representation. *Educational Researcher*, *26*(6), 4–10.

Eliade, M. (1961). *The sacred and the profane: The nature of religion* (W. R. Trask, Trans.). Harper Torchbooks.

Eliade, M. (1964). *Shamanism: Archaic techniques of ecstasy* (W. R. Trask, Trans.). Pantheon.

Eliot, T. S. (2024, February 27). *Little Gidding. T. S. Eliot's* Little Gidding. http://www.columbia.edu/itc/history/winter/w3206/edit/tseliotlittlegidding.html

Ferrini, V. (1991). *Know fish: Books VI and VII*. University of Connecticut Library.

Feynman, R. (1967). *The character of physical law*. MIT Press.

Feynman, R. (1969). What is science? *The Physics Teacher*, *7*(6), 313–320.

Feynman, R. (2025, February 24). *Richard Feynman on pseudoscience* [Video]. YouTube. https://www.youtube.com/watch?v=tWr39Q9vBgo

Fish, B. J. (2013). Painting research: Challenges and opportunities of intimacy and depth. *Journal of Applied Arts & Health*, *4*(1), 105–115. https://doi.org/10.1386/jaah.4.1.105_1

Fish, B. J. (2016). *Art-based supervision: Cultivating therapeutic insight through imagery*. Routledge.

Frankenthaler, H. (2024, February 23). *Helen Frankenthaler, a brief biography*. Helen Frankenthaler Foundation. https://www.frankenthalerfoundation.org/helen/biography

Frayling, C. (1993/1994). Research in art and design. *Royal College of Art Research Papers*, *1*(1), 1–5.

Gadamer, H. (1994). *Truth and method* (2nd rev. ed., J. Weinsheimer & D. G. Marshall, Trans.). Continuum.

Garcia, B. (2025, October 22). *Thriller* (original upload) [Video]. YouTube. https://www.youtube.com/watch?v=hMnk7lh9M3o

Gray, J. (2024, March 25). *Art therapy at Danvers*. Danvers State Hospital. https://www.danversstatehospital.org/art-therapy

Hedlund Nelson, M. (2020). *Art, movement and the body: An art-based research exploration of slow, gentle, and repetitive painting* [Doctoral dissertation, Lesley University]. https://digitalcommons.lesley.edu/expressive_dissertations/99

Heron, J., & Reason, P. (1997). A participatory inquiry paradigm. *Qualitative Inquiry*, *3*(3), 274–294.

Hervey, L. W. (2000). *Artistic inquiry in dance/movement therapy*. Charles C Thomas.

Hill, A. (1945). *Art versus illness: A story of art therapy*. George Allen and Unwin.

Hillman, J. (1977). *Re-visioning psychology*. Harper & Row.

Hillman, J. (1978). *The myth of analysis: Three essays in archetypal psychology*. Harper & Row.

Hillman, J. (1980). *Egalitarian typologies versus the perception of the unique*. Spring Publications (Lecture presented at the 1976 Eranos Conference, Ascona, Switzerland).

Hillman, J. (1983). *Healing fiction*. Station Hill Press.

Hillman, J. (1995). *Kinds of power: A guide to its intelligent use*. Doubleday.

Holton, G. (1994). *Science and anti-science*. Harvard University Press.

Ito, R. (2021). *Tanden art-making as contemplative practice* [Doctoral dissertation, Lesley University]. https://digitalcommons.lesley.edu/expressive_dissertations/111

James, W. (2025, October 22). *The consciousness of lost limbs by William James (1887)*. Classics in the History of Psychology. https://psychclassics.yorku.ca/James/lostlimbs.htm

Jung, C. G. (2009). *The red book: Liber novus* (S. Shamdasani, Ed. & M. Kyburz & J. Peck, Trans.). W. W. Norton.

Kalmanowitz D., & Lloyd B. (1997). *The portable studio: Art therapy and political conflict: Initiatives in the former Yugoslavia and KwaZulu-Natal, South Africa*. Health Education Authority.

Kalmanowitz, D., & Lloyd, B. (Eds.). (2004). *Art therapy and political violence: With art, without illusion*. Routledge.

Kaplan, H., Qandil, L., & Wilkinson, W. (2024, September 22). *How art heals: Integrating practice and research*. London Art Therapy Centre. https://arttherapycentre.com/galleries/video-how-art-heals-integrating-practice-and-research-prof-shaun-mcniff/

Knowles, J. G., & Cole, A. L. (Eds.). (2008). *Handbook of the arts in qualitative research: Perspectives, methodologies, examples, and issues*. Sage.

Koenig, R., & Shaffer, B. (Eds.). (2019). *Eye eye nose mouth: Art, disability, and mental illness in Nanjing, China and Shiga-Ken, Japan*. Harvard University Asia Center & Blurb Publishing.

Kossak, M. (2008). *Attunement: Embodied transcendent experience explored through sound and rhythmic improvisation* (Order No. 3295954) [Doctoral dissertation, Union Institute and University]. ProQuest Dissertations & Theses Global.

Kossak, M. (2012). Art-based enquiry: It's what we do! *Journal of Applied Arts & Health*, *3*(1), 21–29. https://doi.org/10.1386/jaah.3.1.21_1

Kossak, M. (2018). A different way of knowing: Assessment and feedback in art-based research. In R. W. Prior (Ed.), *Using art as research in learning and teaching* (pp. 61–74). Intellect and University of Chicago Press.

Kossak, M. (2021). *Attunement in expressive arts therapy: Toward an understanding of embodied empathy* (2nd ed.). Charles C Thomas.

Kossak, M. (2025). Editorial. *Journal of Applied Arts & Health*, *16*(1), 3–10. https://doi.org/10.1386/jaah_00196_2

Langer, S. K. (1951). *Philosophy in a new key: A study in the symbolism of reason, rite, and art*. Mentor Books.

Langer, S. K. (1957). *Problems of art: Ten philosophical lectures*. Charles Scribner's Sons.

Langer, S. K. (1967). *Mind: An essay on human feeling* (Vol. 1). Johns Hopkins University Press.

Lastoe, S. (2024, March 27). Free portrait project shines a light on South Brooklyn, one painting at a time. *BK Mag*.

https://www.bkmag.com/2023/06/19/free-portrait-project-shines-a-light-on-south-brooklyn-one-painting-at-a-time/

Leavy, P. (2009). *Method meets art: Arts-based research practice*. Guilford Press.

Leavy, P. (Ed.). (2018). *Handbook of arts-based research* (1st ed.). Guilford Press.

Leavy, P. (Ed.). (2025). *Handbook of arts-based research* (2nd ed.). Guilford Press.

Le Guin, U. (1989). *The language of the night: Essays on writing, science fiction, and fantasy*. Scribner.

Lett, W. (2016). *Creative arts companioning in coconstruction of meanings*. Warren Lett.

Lett, W., Fox, K., & von der Borch, D. (2014). Process as value in collaborative arts-based inquiry. *Journal of Applied Arts & Health*, *5*(2), 209–218.

Lev, M. (2019). *Painting intimacy: Art-based research of intimacy* [Doctoral dissertation, Lesley University]. https://digitalcommons.lesley.edu/expressive_dissertations/60

Levinas, E. (1969). *Totality and infinity* (A. Lingis, Trans.). Duquesne University Press.

Levitt, M., & Shapiro, A. (2024, April 23). ISIS destroyed his instruments. He made a new one from scraps and composed an album. *NPR*. https://www.npr.org/2024/04/16/1242389900/ameen-mokdad-music-musician-iraq-mosul-isis

Lewin, K. (1943). Defining the "field at a given time." *Psychological Review*, *50*(3), 292–310.

Lewin, K. (1946). Action research and minority problems. *Journal of Social Issues*, *2*(4), 34–46.

Liamputtong, P., & Rumbold, J. (Eds.). (2008). *Knowing differently: Arts-based and collaborative research methods*. Nova Science.

Liberman, A. (1956). Atelier of Pablo Picasso. *Vogue*, November 1, pp. 156–157.

MacIntyre, A. (2007). *After virtue: A study in moral theory* (3rd ed.). University of Notre Dame Press.

Måndotter, L. (2024). *The song of the soul: The transpersonal dimension of psyche and sound*. Chiron.

Mateus-Berr, R. (2021). Creating an empathetic society for dementia through art: Art, social design and artistic research. In R. Mateus-Berr & L. V. Gruber (Eds.), *Arts and dementia* (pp. 100–153). De Gruyter.

Mateus-Berr, R. (2023). The language of inner experience is art: Participation mystique—Art-based research approaches. *Journal of Applied Arts & Health*, *14*(3), 343–362. https://doi.org/10.1386/jaah_00146_1

Mateus-Berr, R., & Gruber, L. V. (Eds.). (2021). *Arts and dementia*. De Gruyter.

Mateus-Berr, R., & Jochum, R. (Eds.). (2020). *Teaching artistic research*. De Gruyter.

Mateus-Berr, R. et al. (2025, May 30). *Demedarts project catalog: Dementia. Empathy. Education. Arts. Artistic research* (1st ed., 2024). Demedarts. https://www.demedarts.com/kunst

McDonald, A. A. (2025, March 23). Yale School of Art exhibition examines impact of Josef Albers' art and teaching. *Yale News*. https://news.yale.edu/2015/09/01/yale-school-art-exhibition-examines-impact-josef-albers-art-and-teaching

McLuhan, M. (1964), *Understanding media: The extensions of man*. Mentor.

McNiff, S. (1972). *Art therapy at Danvers: A special exhibition of the art made by patients at the Danvers State Hospital, Hathorne, Massachusetts, December 4–31*. Addison Gallery of American Art.

McNiff, S. (1973). A new perspective in group art therapy. *Art Psychotherapy, 1*(3–4), 243–245.

McNiff, S. (1974). *Art therapy at Danvers*. Addison Gallery of American Art. https://www.danversstatehospital.org/art-therapy

McNiff, S. (1975a). Anthony: A study in parallel artistic and personal development. *American Journal of Art Therapy, 14*(4), 126–131.

McNiff, S. (1975b). *A study of motivation in art—Symposium on psychology and the artistic process: Implications for teaching* [Conference presentation]. 83rd annual convention of the American Psychological Association Annual Convention, Chicago, IL, United States.

McNiff, S. (1977). Motivation in art. *Art Psychotherapy, 4*(3–4), 125–136.

McNiff, S. (1979). From shamanism to art therapy. *Art Psychotherapy, 6*(3), 155–161.

McNiff, S. (1981a). *The arts and psychotherapy*. Charles C Thomas.

McNiff, S. (1981b). Video enactment in the expressive therapies. In J. Fryrear & B. Fleshman (Eds.), *Videotherapy in mental health* (pp. 79–92). Charles C. Thomas.

McNiff, S. (1982). Working with everything we have. *American Journal of Art Therapy, 21*(4), 122–123.

McNiff, S. (1986a). Freedom of research and artistic inquiry. *The Arts in Psychotherapy, 13*(4), 279–284.

McNiff, S. (1986b). *Educating the creative arts therapist: A profile of the profession*. Charles C Thomas.

McNiff, S. (1987). Research and scholarship in the creative arts therapies. *The Arts in Psychotherapy*, *14*(2), 285–292.

McNiff, S. (1988). *Fundamentals of art therapy*. Charles C Thomas.

McNiff, S. (1989). *Depth psychology of art*. Charles C Thomas.

McNiff, S. (1992). *Art as medicine: Creating a therapy of the imagination*. Shambhala Publications.

McNiff, S. (1993). The authority of experience. *The Arts in Psychotherapy*, *20*(1), 3–9.

McNiff, S. (1998a). *Art-based research*. Jessica Kingsley Publishers.

McNiff, S. (1998b). *Trust the process: An artist's guide to letting go*. Shambhala Publications.

McNiff, S. (2002). Creating outside the lines: Enlarging psychological research through the arts. *Bulletin of Psychology and the Arts*, *2*(2), 56–59.

McNiff, S. (2003). *Creating with others: The practice of imagination in art, life and the workplace*. Shambhala Publications.

McNiff, S. (2004). Foreword. In D. Kalmanowitz & B. Lloyd (Eds.), *Art therapy and political violence: With art, without illusion* (pp. xii–xvi). Routledge.

McNiff, S. (2007). Knowing Rudolf Arnheim (1904–2007). *Art Therapy: Journal of the American Art Therapy Association*, *24*(3), 138–142.

McNiff, S. (2009). *Integrating the arts in therapy: History, theory, and practice*. Charles C Thomas.

McNiff, S. (2011). Review of *The red book: Liber novus,* by C. G. Jung. In S. Shamdasani (Ed.), M. Kyburz & J. Peck (Trans.). *Art*

Therapy: Journal of the American Art Therapy Association, 28(3), 145–146.

McNiff, S. (Ed.). (2013). *Art as research: Opportunities and challenges*. Intellect and University of Chicago Press.

McNiff, S. (2014a). Art speaking for itself: Evidence that inspires and convinces. *Journal of Applied Arts & Health, 5*(2), 255–262.

McNiff, S. (2014b). Presentations that look and feel like the arts in therapy: Keeping creative tension with psychology. *Australian and New Zealand Journal of Arts Therapy, 9*(1), 89–94.

McNiff, S. (2014c). The role of witnessing and immersion in the moment of arts therapy experience. In L. Rappaport (Ed.), *Mindfulness and the arts therapies: Theory and practice* (pp. 38–50). Jessica Kingsley Publishers.

McNiff, S. (2015). *Imagination in action: Secrets for unleashing creative expression*. Shambhala Publications.

McNiff, S. (2018a). Doing art-based research: An advising vignette. In R. W. Prior (Ed.), *Using art as research in learning and teaching* (pp. 77–89). Intellect and University of Chicago Press.

McNiff, S. (2018b). Creating lives through art: An introduction to outsider art in China with reflections on *Outsider art: Visionary worlds and trauma* by Daniel Wojcik. *Creative Arts in Education and Therapy: Eastern and Western Perspectives, 4*(1), 3–9. https://caet.inspirees.com/caetojsjournals/index.php/caet/article/view/95

McNiff, S. (2018c). Using digital media in art-based research. In C. Malchiodi (Ed.), *The handbook of art therapy and digital technology* (pp. 333–348). Jessica Kingsley Publishers.

McNiff, S. (2019a, August 7–10). *Art is the evidence: Making the case for convincing public communication* [Conference presentation]. "Building Bridges" in Applied Arts & Health, Education and

Community: From the Past to the Present and Future Celebrating 10 Years of the *Journal of Applied Arts & Health*, Telford, UK.

McNiff, S. (2019b). Reflections on what "art" does in art therapy practice and research. *Art Therapy: Journal of the American Art Therapy Association*, *36*(3), 162–165. https://doi.org/10.1080/07421656.2019.1649547

McNiff, S. (2021a). Natural experiments: Researching life through art. *Journal of Applied Arts & Health*, *12*(3), 249–257. https://doi.org/10.1386/ jaah_00074_1

McNiff, S. (2021b). "Companioning" in artistic inquiry: The practice & vision of Warren Lett (1935–2019) & the role of personal process in research. *Journal of Applied Arts & Health*, *12*(1), 45–55. https://doi.org/10.1386/jaah_00056_1

McNiff, S. (2022). Art is the evidence: Convincing public communication of art-based research and its outcomes. In R. W. Prior, M. Kossak, & T. A. Fisher (Eds.), *Applied arts and health, education, and community: Building bridges* (pp. 16–30). Intellect and University of Chicago Press.

McNiff, S. (2023a). Postscript to "Tears on the flowers": Worldwide natural experiments of art healing (2020). *Creative Arts in Education and Therapy—Eastern and Western Perspectives*, *9*(1), 5–9. https://doi.org/10.15212/CAET/2023/9/1

McNiff, S. (2023b). The beauty of authentic and natural expression: Revisiting Rilke & the terrifying beauty of creating anew, 2006. *POIESIS: A Journal of the Arts and Communication*, *20*, 158–164.

McNiff, S. (2023c). The terrifying beauty of creating anew. *POIESIS: A Journal of the Arts and Communication*, *20*, 165–170.

McNiff, S. (2023d). An integral community of art and healing: Transcending silos in the ecological era. *Journal of Applied Arts & Health*, *14*(1), 13–25. https://doi.org/10.1386/jaah_00124_1

McNiff, S. (2024, February 9). *How art heals: Tribute to Terrence Netter*. Pollock-Krasner House. YouTube. https://www.youtube.com/watch?v=bctNzBhbZ84

McNiff, S. (2025). Ecology of creation: Reflections on art as a force of nature. *Journal of Applied Arts & Health, 16*(2–3), 161–173. https://doi.org/10.1386/jaah_00199_1n

McNiff, S., & Coles, R. (1976). Art, artists and psychotherapy: A conversation with Robert Coles. *Art Psychotherapy, 3*(3–4), 115–133.

McNiff, S., & Cook, C. (1975). Video art therapy. *Art Psychotherapy, 2*(1), 55–63.

McNiff, S., Koenig, R., & Shaffer, B. (2019). An Interview with Raphael Koenig and Benny Shaffer: Expanding normality at the edges of the art world in China and Japan. *Creative Arts in Education and Therapy: Eastern and Western Perspectives, 5*(1), 13–24. https://caet.inspirees.com/caetojsjournals/index.php/caet/article/view/170/189

McNiff, S, & Wojcik, D. (2018). A dialogue with Daniel Wojcik on "grassroots" artistic expression and its redemptive power. *Creative Arts in Education and Therapy: Eastern and Western Perspectives, 4*(1), 26–37. http://caet.inspirees.com/caetojsjournals/index.php/caet/article/view/97/109

Miller, A. (2020). *One-canvas method: Art making that transforms on one surface over a sustained period of time* [Doctoral dissertation, Lesley University]. https://digitalcommons.lesley.edu/expressive_dissertations/94

Monk, R. (1999). Wittgenstein's forgotten lesson. *Prospect*. https://www.prospectmagazine.co.uk/regulars/55561/wittgensteins-forgotten-lesson

Moon, B. (1990). *Existential art therapy: The canvas mirror*. Charles C Thomas.

Moon, B. (1992). *Essentials of art therapy training and practice.* Charles C Thomas.

Moon, B. (1999). The tears make me paint: The role of responsive artmaking in adolescent art therapy. *Art Therapy: Journal of the American Art Therapy Association*, *16*(2), 78–82. https//doi.org/10.1080/07421656.1999.10129671

Moon, B. (2010). *Art is life is art: The life and work of Don Jones.* YouTube. https://www.youtube.com/watch?v=JZgpk1EvowU

Munch, E. (2024, February 8). *Edvard Munch.* Quotes of famous people. https://quotepark.com/quotes/1908227-edvard-munch-when-i-write-these-notes-it-is-not-to-describe-my/ (Originally written after 1908 in *The Mad Poet's Diary*, T 2734, 1896–1930).

Musick, P. (2024, November 15). *Pat Musick papers, 1943–2010.* Division of Rare and Manuscript Collections Cornell University Library. http://rmc.library.cornell.edu/EAD/htmldocs/RMM06834.html#d1e143

Nash, G. (2019), Response art in art therapy practice and research with a focus on reflect piece imagery. *International Journal of Art Therapy*, *25*(1), 39–48. https://doi.org/10.1080/17454832.2019.1697307

Nash, G. (2022), Integrative research: Using art to research art. In C. L. Vaculik & G. Nash (Eds.), *Integrative arts psychotherapy* (pp. 196–208). Routledge.

Nelson, R. (2013). *Practice as research in the arts: Principles, protocols, pedagogies, resistances.* Palgrave Macmillan.

Netter, T. (2024, February 9). Terrence Netter. https://www.terencenetter.com/

Newham, P. (1993). *The singing cure: An introduction to voice movement therapy.* Shambhala Publications.

Newham, P. (1998). *Therapeutic voicework: Principles and practices for use of singing as a therapy.* Jessica Kingsley Publishers.

Newsome, B., & Silver, A. (Eds.). (1977). The Addison Gallery of American Art: Video for special audiences. In *The art museum as educator: A collection of studies as guides to practice and policy* (pp. 170–176). University of California Press.

O'Connor, F. (1969). *Mystery and manners: Occasional prose* (S. Fitzgerald & R. Fitzgerald, Eds.). Farrar, Straus and Giroux.

Olson, C. (1951). *Origin: A quarterly for the creative*, Spring (1).

Orlinsky, D. (2024, February 10). Comments on the state of psychotherapy research (as I see it). *Existenzanalyse*. https://www.existenzanalyse.org/wp-content/uploads/Comment_on_the_State.pdf (Originally published in the January 2006 issue of the *NASPR Newsletter*, Society for Psychotherapy Research North American chapter).

Popova, M. (2024, March 3). Martha Graham on the life-force of creativity and the divine dissatisfaction of being an artist. *The Marginalian*. https://www.themarginalian.org/2015/10/02/martha-graham-creativity-divine-dissatisfaction/

Postman, N. (1984). Social science as theology. *ETC: A Review of General Semantics*, *41*(1), 22–3.

Potash, J. (2013). A more complete knowing: The subjective objective partnership. *Journal of Applied Arts & Health*, *4*(1), 49–56. https://doi.org/10.1386/jaah.4.1.49_1

Prinzhorn, H. (1972). *Artistry of the mentally ill*. Springer-Verlag (Original work published 1922 as *Bildnerei der geisteskranken*).

Prior, R. W. (2010). Editorial. *Journal of Applied Arts & Health*, *1*(1), 3–6. https://doi.org/10.1386/jaah.1.1.3/2

Prior, R. W. (2012). *Teaching actors: Knowledge transfer in actor training*. Intellect and University of Chicago Press.

Prior, R. W. (2018a), Art as the topic, process and outcome of research within higher education. In R. W. Prior (Ed.), *Using art as research in learning and teaching* (pp. 43–60). Intellect and University of Chicago Press.

Prior, R. W. (Ed.). (2018b). *Using art as research in learning and teaching*. Intellect and University of Chicago Press.

Prior, R. W., & Kossak, M. (2019). Editorial. *Journal of Applied Arts & Health, 10*(3), 271–276. https://doi.org/10.1386/jaah_00001_2

Prior, R. W., Kossak, M., & Fisher, T. A. (Eds.). (2022). *Applied arts and health, education, and community: Building bridges*. Intellect and University of Chicago Press.

Rank, O. (1968). *Art and artists*. Agathon.

Reason, P. (1999). Integrating action and reflection through co-operative inquiry. *Management Learning, 30*(2), 207–226.

Rennie, D. L., Watson, K. D., & Monteiro, A. M. (2002). The rise of qualitative research in psychology. *Canadian Psychology, 43*, 179–189. https:lfdoi.org/10.1037/h0086914

Richards, M. C. (1989). *Centering in pottery, poetry, and the person* (2nd ed.). Wesleyan University Press (Original work published 1964).

Richter, J. P. (1973). *Horn of Oberon: Jean Paul Richter's school for aesthetics* (M. R. Hale, Trans.). Wayne State University Press (Original work published 1804 as *Vorschule der aesthetik*).

Roethke, T. (2023, January 17). *In a dark time*. Poetry Foundation. https://www.poetryfoundation.org/poems/43347/in-a-dark-time

Rogers, C. (1978). The formative tendency. *Journal of Humanistic Psychology, 18*(1), 23–26.

Rubin, J., & Irwin, E. (2024, October 25). *Videos: Expressive media arts therapies*. psychotherapy.net.

https://www.psychotherapy.net/videos/approach/expressive-media-arts-therapies

Rukeyser, M. (1996). *The life of poetry*. Wesleyan University Press/Paris Press Edition (Original work published 1949).

Rumbold, J., Fenner, P., & Rumbold B. (2014). Special issue: Evidence in a different form. *Journal of Applied Arts & Health*, *5*(2), 163–292.

Salomon, C. (1981). *Charlotte: Life or theater?* (L. Vennewitz, Trans.). Viking.

Saltz, J. (2023, January 17). Out of the erotic ghetto: The Whitney's welcome retrospective rescues Georgia O'Keeffe from sex and flowers. *New York Magazine*. http://nymag.com/arts/art/reviews/59249/

Schafer, W. (Ed.). (1989). *The Truman Nelson reader*. University of Massachusetts Press.

Shapiro, A., Troop, W., & Levitt, M. (2024, March 27). "Music is a need for me" why this violinist composed an album under ISIS. *All Things Considered, NPR*. https://www.npr.org/2024/03/27/1241269513/-music-is-a-need-for-me-why-this-violinist-composed-an-album-under-isis

Shushan, C. (2018). Outsider art in China—An interview with Guo Haiping. *Creative Arts in Education and Therapy (CAET)*, *4*(1), 10–25. https://doi.org/10.15212/CAET/2018/4/3

Simoneaux, G. (2025, February 20). Ambassadors of hope. *Harrambee Arts*. https://www.harambeearts.org/

Skinner, B. F. (1968). *Walden two*. The Macmillan Company (Original work published 1948).

Skinner, B. F. (1971). *Beyond freedom and dignity*. Knopf.

Skinner, B. F. (1972). A lecture on “having” a poem. In B. F. Skinner, *Cumulative record: A selection of papers* (3rd ed., pp. 345–255). Appleton-Century Crofts.

Sontag, S. (1966). *Against interpretation and other essays*. Farrar, Straus and Giroux.

St. Pierre, E. A. (2021). Why post qualitative inquiry? *Qualitative Inquiry, 27*(2): 163–166. https://doi.org/10.1177/1077800420931142

Sullivan, G. (2004). *Art practice as research: Inquiry in visual arts*. Sage.

Suzuki, S. (1989). *Zen mind: Beginner’s mind*. Weatherhill.

Uher J. (2021). Psychology’s status as a science: Peculiarities and intrinsic challenges. Moving beyond its current deadlock towards conceptual integration. *Integrative Psychological and Behavioral Science, 55*(1), 212–224. https://doi.org/10.10 07/s12124-020-09545-0

United Kingdom Department of Health & Arts Council England. (2024, November 15). *Prospectus for arts and health*. Arts Council England. https://www.artsandhealth.ie/wp-content/uploads/2011/09/A-prospectus-for-Arts-Health-Arts-Council-England.pdf

United Kingdom Science Council. (2025, July 15). *Our definition of science*. https://sciencecouncil.org/about-science/our-definition-of-science/

Wei-Ming, T. (1993). *Confucian thought: Selfhood as creative transformation*. State University of New York Press.

Wertz, F. (2014). Qualitative inquiry in the history of psychology. *Qualitative Psychology, 1*(1), 4–16.

White, H. (1985). *Tropics of discourse: Essays in cultural criticism*. The Johns Hopkins University Press.

Whitehead, A. N. (1979). *Process and reality* (2nd ed.). The Free Press.

Whitfield, J. (2024, October 9). How Tyree Guyton's Heidelberg Project helped revitalize Detroit. *Frieze*. https://www.frieze.com/article/how-tyree-guytons-heidelberg-project-helped-revitalize-detroit

Whyte, L. (1974). *The universe of experience*. Harper and Row.

Wilkins, A. (2024, March 29). Mathematician wins 2024 Abel prize for making sense of randomness. *New Scientist*. https://www.newscientist.com/article/2423192-mathematician-wins-2024-abel-prize-for-making-sense-of-randomness/

Wittgenstein, L. (1953). *Philosophical investigations* (G. E. M. Ansombe, Trans.). Basil Blackwell.

Wojcik, D. (2016). *Outsider art: Visionary worlds and trauma*. University Press of Mississippi.

World Health Organization. (2024, November 18). *What is the evidence on the role of the arts in improving health and well-being? A scoping review*. World Health Organization, Europe. https://www.who.int/europe/publications/i/item/9789289054553

Zagaria, A., Andò, A., & Zennaro, A. (2020). Psychology: A giant with feet of clay. *Integrative Psychological & Behavioral Science*, *54*(3), 521–562. https://doi.org/10.1007/s12124-020-09524-5

Index